Wing Chun

Writings for Advanced Practitioners

An Anthology of Articles from the *Journal of Asian Martial Arts*

Compiled by Michael A. DeMarco, M.A.

Copyright © 2016
by Via Media Publishing Company
941 Calle Mejia #822, Santa Fe, NM 87501 USA
E-mail: md@goviamedia.com

All articles in this anthology were originally
published in the *Journal of Asian Martial Arts*.
Listed according to the table of contents for this anthology:

Chaudhuri, J. (2007), Vol. 16 No. 4, pp. 54-65
Webb, J. (2007), Vol. 16, No. 2, pp. 62-81
Chaudhuri, J. (1995), Vol. 4 No. 4, pp. 70-83
Webb, J. (2011), Vol. 20, No. 2, pp. 36-55
Webb, J. (2009), Vol. 18, No. 2, pp. 44-59
Chaudhuri, J. (2012), In *Asian Martial Arts:*
Constructive Thoughts & Practical Applications, pp. 58-61
Webb, J. (2012), In *Asian Martial Arts:*
Constructive Thoughts & Practical Applications, pp. 136-139

Book and cover design
by Via Media Publishing Company
Edited by Michael A. DeMarco, M.A.

Cover illustration

Double-knives flow with precision in the hands of Jeff Webb,
founder the National Ving Tsun Organization (www.nationalvt.com).
Photography by Stephanie Bolin Craft.

ISBN: 9781893765344

contents

CHAPTERS

AUTHORS' BIONOTES

◆ **Dr. Joyotpaul "Joy" Chaudhuri** is a Professor Emeritus of Political Science (political philosophy) at Arizona State University at the Tempe main campus. He has had a life long interest in Asian martial arts as well as martial sports. A longtime student of Augustine Fong, Dr. Caudhuri teaches Wing Chun at Tempe Wing Chun.

◆ **Jeff Webb**, began studying wing chun / ving tsun in 1985 and is a former private student of Grandmaster Leung Ting. During his time in Europe, he also trained under Grandmaster Keith Kernspecht and with numerous masters of the EWTO. Upon his discharge from the military in 1996, Mr. Webb returned to Texas and began teaching the art professionally. In 2005, Mr. Webb was conferred the rank of master by his teacher during a formal grading ceremony in Hong Kong. Later he went on to found the National Ving Tsun Organization in 2007 and continues to operate two professional schools in Austin, Texas. At present he continues to promote the art on a national level and remains a popular instructor on the seminar circuit.

preface

This particular anthology on wing chun features only two authors: Dr. Joyotpaul Chaudhuri and Jeff Webb. Their academic and practical experience bring a rich text for anyone interested in this unique art, famed for its specialized training methods, combative efficiency, and noted associations with Yip Man, Bruce Lee, and the kung fu film industry.

Wing chun is a southern Chinese system, so usually terms are written to reflect Cantonese, often using different romanization systems or mixtures of these systems. On top of this hodgepodge, politics among leading wing chun figures have brought preferences for specific spellings to reflect their unique branches in the wing chun evolutionary tree. Because of this, I have not standardized the romanization in this anthology, as it does not greatly effect the reading.

In chapter one, Dr. Chaudhuri analyzes the keys to motion in the second empty-hand form of wing chun: the bridge seeking routine. The focus is on the proper maintenance of the body's central axis and its motions, which helps with developing the foundations for delivering power.

In the following chapter, Jeff Webb discusses the structure and body mechanics of punching techniques, plus various training methods employed for developing power. Also, punching strategy is shown as the greatest factor in differentiating these punches from those of other styles.

Chaudhuri then analyzes the structure and function of the primary stance in wing chun's first form (sil lim tao), which instills the relational structure of bone, ligament, joint, tendon, muscle, line and angle, while also teaching the inner virtues of softness, stillness, sinking and emptiness.

Two following chapters are by Jeff Webb. The ability to apply martial art techniques at a high rate of speed is essential to overall fighting effectiveness. By looking beyond the physical to the conceptual, he details wing chun's theories that reveal proper timing to be a significant multiplier. His final piece describes both the fundamental and complex methods of "sticking hands" training in detail. It also explains the rationale and theories behind this method as well as discusses a variety of factors that can either improve or retard the acquisition of tactile reflexes. The final two chapters by Chuadhuri and Webb presents some of their favorite techniques.

The content of these chapters explain wing chun rationale and unique fighting methods, plus provides logic and advice to benefit the practitioner.

Michael A. DeMarco, Publisher
Santa Fe, New Mexico, September 2016

iv

chapter 1

Wing Chun's Chum Kiu Form
A Study in Stability and Mobility

by Joyotpaul "Joy" Chaudhuri, Ph.D.

All photographs courtesy of J. Chaudhuri.

"Chum Kiu trains the stance and the waist.
The arm bridge is short and the step is narrow.
Eyes are trained to be alert. The qi flows in perpetual motion."
~ Augustine Fong (n.d.)

Introduction

Differing martial arts systems attempt to address some common problems: the use of the proper engine for power development; developing a delivery system for speed and accuracy; efficient energy use; and proper mind control and spirit. As a southern Chinese art, wing chun has both short- and long-hand motions, but is no exception in its own diligent pursuit of all-round martial development. This chapter's focus is on the concepts of motion in wing chun's second form: *chum kiu* (bridge seeking).

There are different interpretations of the art coming from different lineages. The author's teacher (*sifu*; Man: *shifu*) is Augustine Fong (b. 1950), a distinguished student of Ho Kam Ming of Macao, who was a distinguished student of the late Ip Man (1893-1972) of Fatshan (Man: Foshan) and Hong Kong.

1

The Second Form's Place in Wing Chun

A complete wing chun curriculum would include the three hand forms, the wooden dummy (*mok yang jong*) form, staff (*kwan*), and double knives (*bot jam do*). Each form has applications in various kinds of two-person sticky-hands (*chisao*) timing and motion drills.

The devil, they say, is in the details. The three wing chun forms are loaded with details. One never outgrows the first form,[2] *sil lim tao* (the little idea), which includes much detail on balance, structure, integration, stability, and the key families of hand motions (Chaudhuri, 1995). The wing chun forms are primarily for developing the body, mind, and spirit and the blending of the art's internal and external elements. When the skills are developed in each form, there is a progressive path of development drills. This is accompanied by forms of sticky-hands and crossing-hands (*gor sao*) for testing principles and understanding in each developmental stage.

According to one story, when Ip Man met Leung Bik, son of the great Leung Jan, Leung Bik asked him whether he had learned chum kiu, a significant marker of motion and skill development. Leung Jan, who taught Ip Man's two major teachers, gave a good account of himself in staff usage in Fatshan, the home of a number of gongfu masters, including Wong Fei Hung (1847-1924). Leung Bik reportedly outmaneuvered Ip Man in a contest, then proceeded to teach him wing chun principles and concepts. Weapons work in wing chun is best learned after some mastery of the hands and motion. Unlike some of the Filipino blade and stick arts, wing chun develops the empty-hand motions before introducing the weight of weapons held in the hands. Ip Man blended the harder wing chun he learned from his teacher with a softer version he learned from the son of his teacher's teacher, creating a formidable version of wing chun.

Axis Control

Chum kiu doesn't work well without first having reasonable mastery over the first form, Sil Lim Tao. The form uses a bottom-heavy pyramid structure based on linked triangles to maintain balanced control of the central axis or the mother line. The line runs from the top of the head through the center of the body to the ground and is held in place by the flexible "character two, goat clamping" stance. Slight spinal adjustments help keep the structure stretched enough for energy to flow up and down and to the hands. The axis is related to the spine and meridians, but it has its own importance as the source of balance and harmony with the force of gravity. A good axis is a key to wing chun power. The central axis and yoga's lotus posture (*padma-asana*) are both after the proper gravitational alignment of the spine—one for martial purposes, the other for meditation (*dhyana*). The alignment allows internal energy (*qi* in Chinese-

2

Mandarin or *prana* in Sanskrit) to flow up and down freely. Good axis control is important for directing energy and for the mechanics of motion. After controlling the stillness and balance in wing chun's first form, one is ready for martial motion. Moving on to a dynamic platform involves understanding the turning stance (*chor ma*), the chum kiu form's central stance.

Left: Augustine Fong in the fundamental stance called "two-shaped character, squeezing the goat (Can. *yee gee kim yeung ma*; Man. *er zi qian yang ma*). Right: A small chum kiu turn results in Joy's feet being inside of an attacker's lead foot.

Chor Ma: The Turning Stance

In the turning stance, the vertical axis remains supple but steady and erect and gently stretched without any musculature tightening. All joints work together in the chum kiu turn, or *chor ma*. With the slightest turn, the bottom-heavy wing chun stance can create a speed and power that shoots out through the hands like an arrow in the basic punch or like a snake strike in using the bridge or the fingers.

Proper practice avoids overturning, allowing the stance to take and redirect any pressure or resistance. With practice and guidance, the moves can become subtle and small at close quarters. One also can redirect, defend, or attack per opportunity, intent, and will. Large turns and steps can be used for closing distance or for filling space, or even creating space and repositioning. Wing chun chum kiu motions can be used for shooting in, as well as for close-quarters work.

The turning and stepping motions in the chum kiu turning stance use the entire foot on flat ground in the motion's development stage. Later, one can adjust to rough or soft floors by lifting the foot to avoid stress on the knees. Adjustments link development to application in varying environments. In the ground connection, Ip Man's training used the center of his heels while using the rest of the foot for controlling the ground connection and adjusting balance. The center of the heels provides a pivot point that allows the feet to turn on flat surfaces without being lifted. Controlling with the feet and toes prevents throwing the main axis off. The use of the heels doesn't involve leaning back or forward on them. With training, all of the joints assist in stability and mobility.

Fong in the turning stance (*chor ma*),
allowing a 180-degree directional movement.

The Role of the Shoulders

The best of Ip Man Wing Chun involves square-body work and facing an opponent. There are other styles that use a slanted body. Having a square body allows one to turn 180 degrees on a dime with equal balance on both feet without taking a step. This allows for the hands to be balanced and ready to play together in coordinating defense and attack with near simultaneity. The square body can be helpful for two-handed work such as in the butterfly palms (*po pai*). In addition to the mastery of the turn, the chum kiu form includes several stepping motions. When the turning and stepping are integrated, there is greater power generation. The chum kiu form has a section where one steps up and uses both palms in a forward motion. These two-handed, square-bodied butterfly motions are developed again on the wooden man dummy, so power can be released by the strong, but flexible, structure efficiently and not held back in tightened arm muscles.

The vertical axis and its cleanly circular turning with balanced feet and joint drilling are important ingredients in good chum kiu. The generation of chum kiu power enhances the work of the elbows, which are important energy-origination points (the beginning punch practice, for example) and transmitters for the bridges (*kiu*) and hands. Springy, flexible, and strong elbows provide the key links between the shoulders and wrists. The wing chun concept of the body divides it into six "gates," or doors, if viewed from the front or back. The main vertical axis is crossed by two horizontal axis lines, one at the heart level and one near the groin. Horizontal-leveled chum kiu turns allow for quick movements, permitting the elbows to move from one horizontal or vertical level to another and helping to protect the gates.

In the *chor ma* turn, well-aligned knees, ankles, and toes get the motion going, with the feet and heels on the ground. Without proper alignment, undue stress is placed on the knees. The power generated from the ground torques its way to the waist, where it gets a major boost at the body's center point (*dantin*; Man: *dantian*). A slight spin beginning at the bottom can create a power chain and produce a quick, powerful spin at the top when needed.

The Role of the Waist

The waist plays a vital role in chum kiu, since it connects the footwork to the hands and the upper body. The waist needs to be an important power transmitter. Like many Asian arts, the *dantin* is very important for motion assistance and storing energy. The main dantin lies on the center axis with other energy points up and down the axis. The central axis-based use of the dantin contrasts with the silk reeling *dantin* rotation of Chen style taiji training. The axis rotation assists in the drilling of the joints used in wing chun motion. For wing chun, it is drilling, and for Chen style, it's silk reeling (Man: *chan-sigong*). The power system also is different from karate, which emphasizes the hips, and the shoulder loading of Western boxing crosses and hooks. The center-line orientation of wing chun's chum kiu also makes for straighter and more direct motions than a beginner's Choy Li Fut, which is a style with more swinging punches.

The first form's basic motions go through subtle modifications because of chum kiu's turns and steps. Thus, the guarding hand (*wu sao*) in chum kiu appears to shift from the center of the chest. The appearance is deceptive, because the guarding hand is still on the new line connecting one's axis to that of the other's axis. The axis-to-axis center line remains important but the chum kiu turns can create different angles and options for the elbows to aim the hands at the target.

Further in the development process, in chisao or various sticking-hand drills, subtle variations in positioning the guarding hand, the controlling hand (*fok*), or the wing hand (*bong*) will occur because of the shifts in the centerline dynamics between two people doing sticky hands. Improved eye focus and awareness with stable and balanced, but quick and controlled, chum kiu and sticky hands training leads one further along the path of creative and spontaneous action. The chum kiu turns and steps provide a basis for adjusting to forces coming from all sides. Examples include the chor ma turn, frontal stepping, stepping back, turning and stepping, and joint alignment. All steps are accompanied by hand motions, and there are key kicks in chum kiu, as well.

Above: A chum kiu turn changes hand positions and angles.
Below: Fong's chum kiu turn (note feet) opens a line for a bar arm control and chop. Fong's elbow to ribs as powered by a chum kiu turn.

Close-Quarters Explosive Short Power

The hand motions derived from good chum kiu can deliver explosive short power (*bau ja geng*), wing chun's version of taiji's explosive power (Man: *fajing*) at one inch or less. The better the joint coordination, the better the power delivery. Chum kiu stances and motions also can deliver power when contact is made to the legs. The combined stability and mobility of chum kiu stance work can upset a grappler's balance and platform, diminishing the effectiveness of their hands in shooting for the legs. Sprawling isn't the only possible option in response to a takedown. Changing the power line, attacking, or side-stepping are also possibilities. The key is controlling an individual's vertical axis and the center line or lines between two or more people.

Ho Kam Ming gets impatient when asked about being taken down. He says that, generally, any wing chun practitioner who gets taken down needs to learn or relearn the structural integrity of good sil lim tao and the coordinated and aligned chum kiu forward and turning motions applied instantaneously upon contact.

In addition to stance, footwork, and handwork, there is breathing, looking, and timing. At the chum kiu development stage, distinct chum kiu motions find their way into sticky hands practice. These include piercing, catching, and bar arm. These motions can be used for defending, striking, throwing, or joint control or breaking. The eyes are especially alert in chum kiu, adjusting to rapid motion without losing focus and with the head moving with the body. The breathing is natural and proportionate to the exertion involved. There is no special emphasis on exhalation, shouting, or snorting. Spontaneous and reflexive action directs the energy wherever bridging occurs or is made.

The control of intent; the natural breathing; the sil lim tao body structure; and the chum kiu turns, steps, and other footwork create the wing chun version of the ideal of stillness in motion. The motion can be short, long, and at different speeds and timing, yet follow clear paths to the center of things. There are various forms of power in wing chun, the discussion of which is beyond the scope of this chapter. Chum kiu plays a vital role in all wing chun power development.

As the proverb at the beginning of this chapter points out, chum kiu trains the stance and the waist. The arm bridge is short, and the step is narrow. The eyes are trained to be alert, and the internal energy flows in perpetual motion.

Development and Application

It should be noted that the forms, including chum kiu, are for development in the wing chun art. The sticky hands exercise helps sharpen understanding of the development and forces involved in contact and timing. In actual conflict or application, wing chun strategies, principles, tactics, practice, and experience help adjust and operationally link the development to the unique situations that arise in the real world. In application, a straight punch can be bent at the elbow hinge, though for development, the punch is extended fully. The body's joints, like coordinated springs, can release as much power as necessary, while conserving the rest for more work, flow, or follow-up.

7

Technical Section

The following technical section will demonstrate the practical advantages of using wing chun principles as found in chum kiu. The proper maintenance of the body's central axis and its motions helps with the development of wing chun power and the foundations of delivering that power.

1-a Basic facing postures.
1-b Josh controls Joy's punch with an open-palm deflection.
1-c Joy's turns (chor ma) creating an opening.
1-d He easily continues with a palm strike.

2-a Josh ready for a grappler's adapted Greco-Roman body grab.

2-b Immediately upon grappler's touch, Joy's chor ma dissolves and controls the power of the grabbing motion.

3-a Josh blocks Joy's punch with a boxing guard.

3-b Turning allows Joy to reposition, control, and punch with the other hand.

4-a Josh going for a shoot to the legs.

4-b Joy's chum kiu step and turn motions jams and controls his opponent's center line.

4-c Josh's head is quickly turned with the motion.

5-a Josh prepares to attack.

5-b Josh begins to kick.

5-c Joy advances with butterfly palms, stopping Josh's motion.

5-d Off-balance, Josh begins to fall.

6-a Dana about to punch Joy.
6-b Joy steps in, deflecting using his left hand, and turns to throw a hook to liver.
6-c A follow-up turn and a punch to the kidney.

Right:
Master Augustine Fong with
the author, Joy Chaudhuri.

Conclusion

Wing chun's second form, chum kiu, provides the foundation for wing chun motions without sacrificing the fundamental principles of stability, energy flow, and hand motions that are developed through repeated practice of the first form. The chum kiu form teaches footwork, stepping, turning, coordination for proper kicking and adjusting to shifting lines, and angles or power paths. The form provides keys to training for contact.

GLOSSARY

Characters	Cantonese	Pinyin	English
鏢指	biu jee	biao zhi	shooting fingers
膀手	bong sao	bang shou	elbow up/wing hand
八斬刀	bot jam do	ba zhan dao	eight-slash knives
黐脚	chi gerk	chi jiao	sticky legs
黐手	chisao	chishou	sticky hands
尋橋	chum kiu	xun qiao	seeking the bridge
轉馬	chor ma	zhuan ma	turning stance
丹田	dantin	dantian	"red/cinnabar field"
短橋	dyun kiu	duan qiao	short bridges
佛山	Fatsan	Foshan	Buddhist Mountain
伏手	fuk sao	fu shou	controlling/covering hand
何金銘	Ho Kam Ming	He Jin Ming	(wing chun master)
圈手	huen sao	quan shou	circling hand
葉問	Ip Man	Ye Wen	(wing chun master)
橋	kiu	qiao	bridge
桿	kwan	gan	staff
攔手	lan sao	lan shou	bar arm/hand
梁壁	Leung Bik	Liang Bi	(wing chun master)
梁贊	Leung Jan	Liang Zan	(wing chun master)
拉手	lop sao	la shou	grabbing hand
木人樁	mok yan jong	murenzhuang	wooden man dummy
師父	sifu	shirfu	teacher, instructor
小念頭	sil lim tao	xiao nian tou	the little idea
攤手	tan sao	tan shou	palm up/open and spread
詠春	wing chun	yong chun	forever spring
護手	wu sao	hu shou	defensive/guarding hand

References

Chaudhuri, J. (1995). Defending the motherline, Wing chun's sil lim tao, *Journal of Asian Martial Arts*, 4(4) 70-83.

Fong, A. (n.d.). *The complete system of wing chun gung fu: Wing chun theories and concepts, vol. 7*. Tucson: Fong's Health Center.

Special thanks to the following: Dana Albert for all the photography except for the photo of Master Fong and Joy taken at the Fong Center in Tucson by Fong Wing Chun instructor William Denny; Master Fong for his teaching, writings and pictures; Joshua Santobianco and Dana Albert for helping with the demonstrations; Stephen Morton for the translations of wing chun terms and aphorisms; and Heather Wells for reviewing and editing an early draft.

chapter 2

Analysis of the
Wing Tsun Punching Methods

by Jeff Webb

Professor Leung Ting (Mandarin: Liang Ting) was a disciple of Yip Man in
Hong Kong. Today he is the world-wide grandmaster of the International
Wing Tsun Association. *Photograph courtesy of Leung Ting.*
All photographs courtesy of J. Webb, except where noted.

Introduction

Of the myriad punching techniques available in the martial arts today,
perhaps none are more misunderstood than those of wing tsun gongfu
(Man., *yong chun*). The style's three punching techniques, while few in number,
represent an extremely effective approach to striking with the closed fist. At
first glance, the rather short stroke of these punches would seem disproportionate
to the amount of power they generate. But like all aspects of wing tsun,
precision application plays a more crucial role in one's success than does brute
force. Take for example wing tsun's trademark technique known as "chain
punching." This series of rapid, non-stop straight-line thrusting punches is often
imitated yet seldom duplicated by non-wing tsun stylists. Then there are wing
tsun's lifting punch and hooking punch, which are frequently confused with the
uppercut and the hook from Western boxing.

The purpose of this chapter will be to analyze the three punching techniques of wing tsun. The proper structure and body mechanics of each punch will also be discussed, in addition to the various training methods employed for developing power. Finally, we will examine the strategy for applying the wing tsun punches, which will serve as the greatest factor differentiating them from the punches of other martial arts styles.

A Brief History of Wing Tsun Gongfu

Approximately 250 years ago, a Buddhist nun named Ng Mui (Man., Wu Mei) set out to create a new style of Chinese gongfu which would take advantage of the weak points of the existing Shaolin systems. Being well-versed in the Shaolin arts and an accomplished pugilist in her own right; she sought to distill a number of highly effective movements into a condensed form which could be quickly learned and applied. The resulting method was comprised of narrow, upright stances; utilized deflections and redirections rather than force-on-force blocking; and a relied on a handful of short, powerful strikes. Her creation was soon field-tested in the hands of Yim Wing Tsun (Man., Yan Yongchun), a young woman who was being harassed by a local bully who was intent on marrying her. After learning the foundations of this system from the nun, Yim Wing Tsun was able to defeat the bully and send him on his way. Yim Wing Tsun later married a salt merchant named Leung Bok Chau (Man., Liang Bochou) to whom she had been betrothed since her childhood. Leung quickly saw the merit in his wife's gongfu and learned it for himself, becoming one of the style's early progenitors. Later, whenever he was asked the name of his gongfu style he said "it is Wing Tsun's gongfu," meaning the gongfu of his wife Wing Tsun, whose name translates to mean "Praise Springtime." In the years and decades that followed, wing tsun gongfu was handed down in secrecy from one generation to the next. Each successive generation made contributions to the development of the art and by the 20th century it came under the leadership of Mr. Yip Man (Man., Ye Wen), a wealthy resident of Fatshan (Man., Foshan), China. Fleeing the Communist takeover in the late 1940's, Grandmaster Yip Man brought the art to Hong Kong; where he began teaching gongfu as a profession. For the first time in its history, this once secret style was made available to the general public.

It can be said that Grandmaster Yip Man, although a highly-skilled practitioner himself, was not very enthusiastic about teaching. Already having been retired, and in his mid-fifties before arriving in Hong Kong, Grandmaster Yip Man taught more out of necessity than desire. Despite this fact, it is estimated that thousands of people learned with this famous grandmaster during his teaching career. Of these it was his last student, Leung Ting, who has had the greatest success in spreading wing tsun around the world. Grandmaster

Professor Leung Ting began learning wing tsun in 1960. By the early 1970's he was already a well-known instructor and trainer of full-contact champions. In Hong Kong, his classes grew so quickly that the press dubbed him "the instructor of a million students." On the heels of this success, he began teaching internationally in the mid-seventies. Today, Professor Leung Ting's International Wing Tsun Association (IWTA) spans more than 64 countries and encompasses thousands of schools world-wide.

The Straight-Line Thrusting Punch and Chain Punches

Perhaps the most well-known fighting technique of wing tsun gongfu is the straight-line thrusting punch (*yat-gee-chung-kuen*). The straight-line punch is typically a student's first lesson in wing tsun and, while it is introduced in the "little idea" (*sil nim tao*) practice set, it is also found in the other two empty-hand sets as well as in the wooden dummy routine. This short, jolting strike begins by holding the fist vertically and placing it at the center of the chest. As the punch is thrust outward, it travels forward along the centerline until the arm reaches full extension. Although a single punch can possess a great deal of striking power, these punches are most often applied in a series known as chain punches (*lin-wan-chung-kuen*). Linked together in this fashion, these multiple straight-line thrusting punches can be applied very quickly and with a great deal of power. It is not uncommon for advanced students of wing tsun to average between 5 and 7 chain punches per second.

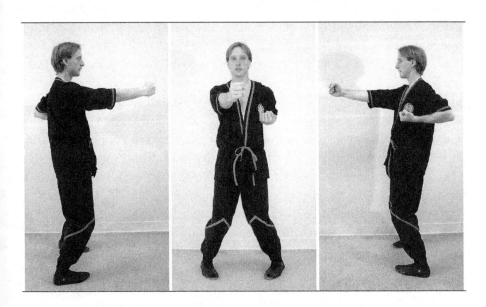

Finished position of straight-line
thrusting punch as viewed from sides and front.

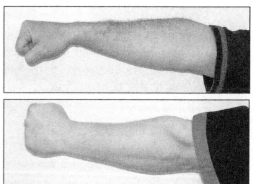

Left: Close-up of the finished position of straight-line thrusting punch. Right: Close-up of fist alignment of the reverse punch (above) and the straight-line punch (left).

The power of this punch relies on three key factors: first, the fist must travel as straight as possible towards its intended target; second, the fist should remain closed but not tightly-clenched, which ensures that the whole arm is loose and relaxed; third, the punch should be thrust out to full extension as quickly as possible. Rapid and full contraction of the triceps generates the acceleration needed to propel the fist forward with explosive power. Quite often, wing tsun experts are approached by other martial artists and asked for a quick lesson in what they call "the wing tsun straight blast." Naturally, there is a proper method for executing the straight-line thrusting punch, but dedicated training and physical development are required to achieve the same effect that a wing tsun expert produces. In any case, to generate a powerful straight-line punch, one must develop powerful fast twitch triceps, strong latissimus dorsi muscles, and most importantly tendon strength in the wrist and elbow joints. Correct muscular development and punching technique are evidenced by a deep, audible snapping sound when a punch is thrown in the air. Most wing tsun practitioners with at least three years of consistent training can achieve this; regardless of whether they are wearing a t-shirt, gongfu jacket, or no top at all. This whiplash effect occurs when the elbow joint locks out and the shoulder recoils. Understandably, this level of development requires dedicated training and proper instruction. Incorrect technique leads to minimal power and potential joint injury. For this reason it is important to seek out a qualified wing tsun instructor.

Along with conditioning the muscles and tendons of the arm itself, development of the fist is of equal importance. In contrast to the typical reverse punch which strikes with the top two knuckles, the wing tsun straight-line thrusting punch uses the bottom three knuckles and the shins of those fingers as well. While focusing one's power in a small area is important, there are diminishing returns to be considered when the striking surface is too small. Of primary concern is whether or not the striking surface is sufficient to transmit 100% of the striking power into the target. Structurally, the wing tsun straight-line thrusting punch provides optimum stability along the line of power. Upon examining the fist and forearm, it is obvious that the middle finger and ring finger are the two digits best supported by the forearm. The small finger (or 'pinkie') comes in a close second while the index finger is least supported by the forearm. Clearly a straight-line punch with the fist held vertically and striking with the bottom three knuckles; presents a more stable striking surface than the standard reverse punch which utilizes the knuckles of the index and middle fingers.

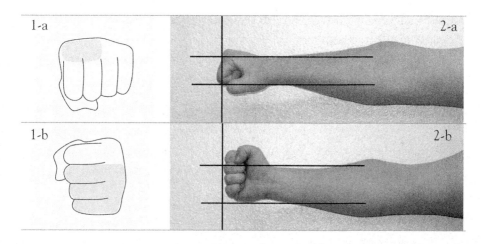

Left: Graphics comparing the striking area of the hand in typical fighting styles (1-a) and that of the wing tsun fist used in a straight-line thrusting punch (1-b).
Right: Wrist alignment in the typical fighting styles (2-a) and that of the wing tsun straight-line punch (2-b).

The straight-line punch can be applied from either a stationary position or while in motion. However, the destructive power of this punch is greatly amplified when combined with wing tsun stepping. By utilizing the principle of addition of velocities, a straight-line thrusting punch applied in coordination with the advancing step (*chin-bo*) effectively puts one's entire body weight behind this strike. Properly executed, three things will occur simultaneously: the fist will contact the target; the elbow will begin extending; and the body-weight will shift in conjunction with the step. In both real-world application and in resistance training against a target, the elbow remains bent until the fist makes contact. At that moment, the elbow will fully extend and delivers its power.

Training Methods for the Straight-Line Thrusting Punch

The exercise known as "air-punching" is the most fundamental for developing powerful straight-line thrusting punches. To begin with the practitioner will position himself in a wing tsun stance and pose the pre-fighting posture with both fists closed. Next, he will launch successive punches in the air, one after the other, beginning with the rear hand. For training purposes, these chain thrusting punches are always thrown in odd numbered quantities such as 1, 3, 5, 7, or 9. Punching in this fashion causes the opposite hand to become the lead hand after each set. To illustrate, if the practitioner begins with the left hand in front and throws 3 punches, the right hand will end up in the lead position. Primarily, this is done to ensure ambidextrous power development. During the chain punching exercise, the hands must always proceed forward in a wrist over wrist manner. This aids in keeping the trajectory straight and also provides maximum protection of the centerline while punching. Some typical air-punching exercises are:

> **Punching in Sets** - On each count, the student will throw a series of 3 or 5 punches. Each count of ten would yield 30 or 50 punches respectively, and ten sets of ten yielding 300 or 500 punches could be considered a good warm-up.

> **Timed Punching** - In this exercise, the student will punch non-stop at full-speed and power for timed rounds of 1 or more minutes. In between rounds the student will rest to allow the muscles to recover. This exercise develops the endurance necessary to deliver continuous, fast, and powerful punches for longer periods during a fight.

> **Focused Punching** - This involves punching against an object such as a lit candle or a suspended sheet of paper. Here, the focused power of the individual punch is emphasized. When punching at the lit candle, the practitioner should position their extended arm several inches from the flame and strive to extinguish the flame by displacing air with their punch. When punching at a sheet of paper, the student will stand so that the extended arm reaches an inch or so past the paper. Here the goal is to strike the paper with increasing amounts power and practice the proper depth of the strike.

Developing Heavy Punches with the Wall Bag

Whereas air-punching develops proper technique, accuracy, and focus; Wall Bag punching develops heavy, knock-down striking power. The wall bag is a square canvas pouch measuring roughly 12" x 12" which is filled with sand or rice and suspended flatly against a strong load-bearing wall. Its purpose is to serve as a cushion between the wing tsun practitioner's fist and a solid immovable object. For this reason, the wall bag should be placed on a wall which can withstand continued powerful striking on a regular basis. It is not uncommon that bricks and mortar will loosen from repeated vibration caused by wall bag punching. When punching on the wall bag, one should be close enough that the arm is slightly bent when the fist is in contact with the bag. Alternating left and right punches are thrown at the center of the wall bag with an emphasis on relaxed, even power. As with air-punching, the fist is closed but not tightly clenched. Upon contact, a properly formed fist compresses upon itself providing a structure which does not require excess tension in the muscles of the forearm. With the whole arm kept loose, the only tension required is a powerful contraction of the triceps—which is essential to launching the punch at great speed.

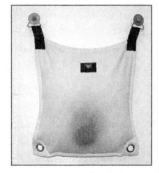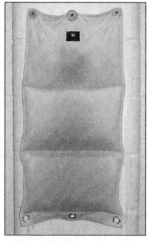

Single (left) and triple section (right)
wall bags mounted on 3/4" plywood
and bolted to a cinder block wall.

The first exercise of wall bag punching is to toughen the skin of the fist. Beginning in a stationary position in front of the wall bag, the practitioner will deliver approximately 20 to 50 individual strikes alternating with the left and right. After each punch has made contact with the bag, the practitioner will pause momentarily and scrape their fist downward against the canvas to condition the skin. Then they will throw the next strike in a similar fashion, and so on. Within several days of this practice, the skin will be tough enough and the scraping action can be eliminated. Beginners can then progress to throwing between two hundred and six hundred punches per day. Patience and diligence are the keys to success. Occasionally some students wanting a short cut to quick results will attempt to do higher repetitions before they are physically ready. While they may be able to throw more punches, the question is whether or not the fist is ready for this. As a result, the skin of the knuckles will often tear and bleed while the flat of the fist may become quite sore. This prevents further training until the injuries are completely healed, otherwise the scabs will break and the knuckles will bleed once again. Some practitioners advocate the use of gloves when punching on the wall bag, but this idea is somewhat backwards. After all, what good is it to develop powerful punches when one's hands are too fragile to wield that power without injury?

Once a student develops the basic ability to punch on the wall bag, they can begin punching in sets. Each set contains 200 punches with the first 50 punches and last 50 punches being thrown slowly and with full power. The intervening 100 punches, however, are thrown at full speed rather than full power. Upon completion of each set, the practitioner will take a break and allow the arms to fully recover before proceeding to the next set. The methodology of using low repetitions and minimizing muscular fatigue are well-known secrets to many of the world's foremost strength experts. Quoting Pavel Tsatsouline, Russian Master of Sports, "Muscle failure is more than unnecessary—it is counterproductive! Neuroscientists have known for half a century that if you stimulate a neural pathway... and the outcome is positive, future [efforts] will be easier, thanks to the so-called Hebbian rule" (2000: 17). The Hebbian rule, proposed by psychologist Donald O. Hebb (1904-1985), essentially states that when any two systems of cells are repeatedly and simultaneously active that they tend to become associated with one another to such an extent that activity in one induces activity in the other. For our purposes this means that muscles that have fully recovered between sets on the wall bag are more likely to contract together, contract quickly, and contract more fully in support of the punching effort. Therefore, the traditional method for punching on the wall bag as passed down by Grandmaster Professor Leung Ting involves sets of 200 punches with adequate recovery time between sets. According to Grandmaster Leung, practitioners wishing to compete in fighting contests are expected to maintain a minimum of 2000 punches per day, divided into 10 sets of 200 punches. The speed and power of the wing tsun straight-line thrusting punch is one of the reasons that Grandmaster Leung's fighters consistently won by knock-out in the popular gongfu contests of the 1970's and 80's in Hong Kong.

Next page, left: Preliminary conditioning of the skin of the fist is accomplished by throwing individual punches (3-a-b); and afterwards scraping the fist downward (3-c) prior to launching the next punch (3-d-e). This process is repeated over and over again.

Chain punching (center) on the wall bag begins by placing one fist on the bag (4-a) and then punching wrist-over-wrist with second fist (4-b-c). The process is then repeated on the other side (4-d-e) and continues by alternating left and right punches.

Double Punching (right) (5-a-d) is the method of applying two straight-line thrusting punches simultaneously at different heights. In application, the opponent's two arms are wedged-out and therefore controlled by the double punches.

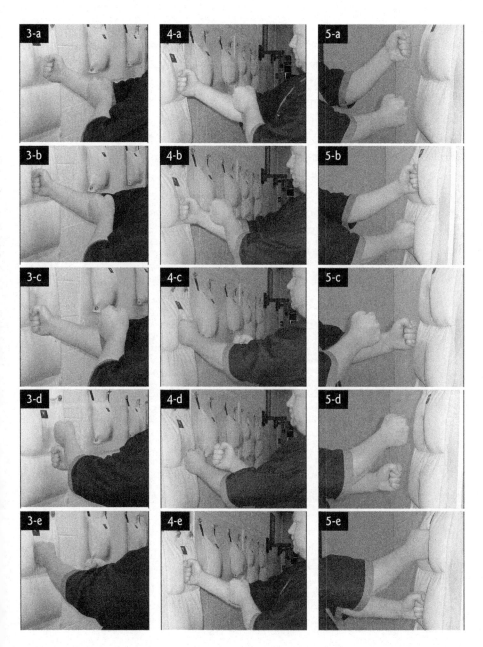

The Lifting Punch

The second of wing tsun's trinity of punches is the "lifting punch" (*chau chong kuen*) which is introduced in wing tsun's intermediate set known as arm-seeking (*chum kiu*). It is applied as a substitute for the straight-line punch under circumstances when a straight punch would not be possible. Although the lifting punch is used less frequently than the straight-line punch, its destructive power should not be underestimated. In actual application, the lifting punch is always augmented by a complimentary controlling technique with the other hand. For example, against an attempted waist grab or clench, the attacker's head would typically be pressed or pulled in the direction of the on-coming lifting punch. Since the lifting punch targets the nose, throat, or lower jaw, such a strike will result in severe injury. This is especially true since the attacker is not afforded the luxury of being able to 'roll' with the punch or otherwise dissipate the impact. To visualize this effect, imagine trying to smash a coconut by striking it with a hammer as you would strike a golf ball. While the impact may be powerful, the coconut can simply roll away with minor damage. However, place the coconut on the concrete floor and hold it firmly in place while the hammer crashes downward and the results are quite different.

Many people often assume that the lifting punch is similar to the boxing uppercut, when in fact the two are quite different in both form and function. The key differences between them are as follows:

TRAJECTORY
- **Uppercut:** Begins close to the abdomen and follows an oblique arc moving first downwards, then upwards.
- **Lifting Punch:** Begins near the center of the chest and follows a tight arc moving upwards.

BODY MOVEMENT
- **Uppercut:** The head stays low and the entire body sinks to one side as the punch dips then rises. Weight is predominantly on the front leg.
- **Lifting Punch:** The head and body both remain upright. The arm movement is accompanied by a short torque of the waist. Weight remains on the rear leg.

TARGETING
- **Uppercut:** Thrown to the body or chin of the opponent while at close-range, the effects are damaging.
- **Lifting Punch:** Thrown to the face, chin, or at the throat of the opponent, the effects are potentially lethal.

FORCE APPLIED

• **Uppercut:** The torque of the body and follow through with the shoulder are combined by pushing off of the rear foot.

• **Lifting Punch:** The upward thrusting movement of the elbow is combined with an upward lifting motion of the spine and a turning motion of the waist. The lifting punch is always applied with a simultaneous wrist grab or a neck pulling maneuver. This prevents the target from retreating with the force of the blow, thus increasing the force of impact with the target.

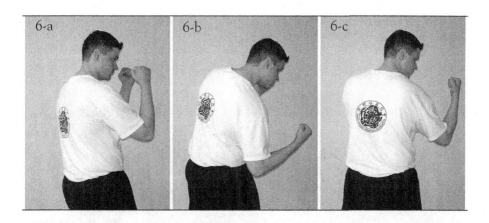

The boxing uppercut begins with lowering the right shoulder (6a-b) and keeping the arm close to the body. As the body turns into the punch, the shoulder, elbow, and fist thrust upward (6c). The elbow should remain at a 90 degree angle during the process to ensure maximum power.

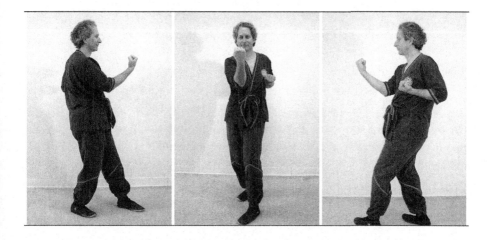

Finished position of lifting punch as viewed from sides and front.

Training Methods for the Lifting Punch

The arm muscles used with the lifting punch are essentially the same as those used with the straight-line thrusting punch since the elbow is first brought close to the centerline, before being thrust forwards and upwards. Therefore physical attainment in the straight-line punch (both in the air and on the wall bag) produces the necessary muscular conditioning.

Further gains in power can be derived from properly coordinating the stance turning movement and the upward lifting motion of the spine. Correct timing and delivery of this movement are essential. This is developed by repetitive practice of the chum kiu form; solo exercises of stance turning with the lifting punch; and most importantly, practice in applying the movements against a live training partner.

Lifting punch with head control to defend against a grapple attack (7-a) and with hand control to defend against a reverse punch (7-b).

The Hooking Punch

Wing tsun's third punch is the hooking punch (au-chong-kuen) and it is introduced in the third empty-hand set called "thrusting fingers" (biu tze). Since the techniques of thrusting fingers require the foundational movements of the previous two forms, it is only taught to advanced students who have skillfully mastered the fighting applications of "little idea" (sil nim tao) and "arm seeking" (chum kiu). In addition to the hooking punch, the thrusting fingers set also introduces a number of potentially lethal striking techniques with the elbows, palms, and fingers. For this reason it was a highly-guarded secret in ancient times. In the present day however, any hard-working student of wing tsun has the opportunity to learn this form after approximately four years of study.

The hooking punch, like the lifting punch, is used only when the straight-line punch is not feasible due to one's relative position to the opponent. In the case of the hooking punch, this arises when the wing tsun practitioner is both at close range and at a perpendicular angle to the opponent. The punch is formed by holding the forearm nearly parallel to the floor with the elbow slightly lower than the wrist. During actual application, the angle of the elbow joint is generally between 90 and 135 degrees and the fist travels horizontally along a very short, almost flat arc. In both the biu tze set and in practical fighting, it is thrown in coordination with a torquing movement of the waist and a whipping motion of the arm. While in the training form this involves turning the stance as well; in actual fighting the hooking punch is often performed without necessarily moving the feet.

Another similarity to the lifting punch is that the hook is always accompanied by a controlling technique. This serves not only to increase the power of the strike, but also prevents the opponent from evading the blow.

There are two primary ways to apply the hooking punch and each method seeks to unbalance the opponent just prior to striking them. The first uses a double grappling hand technique to take hold of the opponent's own on-coming attack and use it to pull them forward. As the opponent is off-balance and stumbling forward, the hooking is thrown in the exact opposite direction creating a powerful head-on collision. By using the opponent's own momentum and coupling that with a torquing movement of the waist during execution, the wing tsun hooking punch produces enormous destructive power. Typical targets for this hooking punch application are the throat, nose, chin and mandible. The second method involves uses a single grappling hand to exploit the opponent's force and pull them off balance while striking them from the side or from behind, rather than head-on. This application of the hooking punch targets either the base of the skull, the ear, temple, or temporomandibular joint. Regardless of which variation of the hooking punch is used, the results are equally incapacitating.

In comparison to the hook punch from Western boxing, the wing tsun hooking punch shares a few minor similarities in appearance, as well as a number of important differences:

FORM
• **Boxing Hook:** Fist is held either vertically with the thumb on top and the small finger on the bottom or with the back of the hand on top and the palm facing downward. Angle of the elbow joint is 90 degrees or greater.

• **Wing Tsun Hooking Punch:** Fist is held exclusively with the back of the hand on top and the palm facing downward. Elbow joint angle is 90 degrees or greater.

25

TRAJECTORY

- **Boxing Hook:** Swings in a relatively wide arc.
- **Wing Tsun Hooking Punch:** Swings in a nearly flat arc.

BODY MOVEMENT

- **Boxing Hook:** The body-weight shifts from left to right or vice-versa as the feet pivot in coordination with the hook.
- **Wing Tsun Hooking Punch:** The body-weight remains on the rear leg while the upper body swivels at the hip. There is little to no movement of the feet.

TARGETING

- **Boxing Hook:** Thrown to the body, face or side of the head.
- **Wing Tsun Hooking Punch:** Thrown to the throat, face, side of the head, or base of the skull.

FORCE APPLIED

- **Boxing Hook:** Uses the torque of the waist and shifting of the stance along with the power of the arm.
- **Wing Tsun Hooking Punch:** Uses the torque of the waist and power of the arm, in conjunction with a controlling technique to pull the opponent off-balance and often directly into the hooking punch.

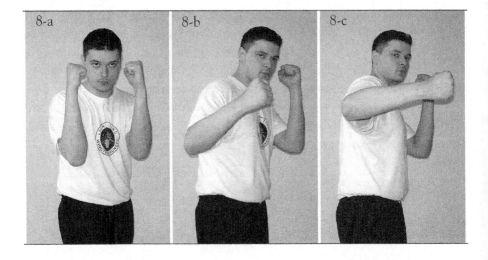

With hands in the ready position, the boxing hook is initiated by turning the body and shifting weight from one foot to the next. Upon completion the right side of the body should be lined up with the direction of the punch (8-a-c).

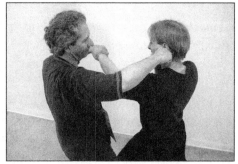

Left: Finished position of a hooking punch. Right: Hooking punch
to the ear with hand control to defend a reverse punch.

Training Methods for the Hooking Punch

The hooking punch is unique among the three wing tsun punches since its elbow position is not on the centerline. Both the straight-line thrusting punch and lifting punch utilize "elbow force," a term which describes the force generated by keeping the elbow close to the centerline. In actuality, this type of elbow force relies primarily on the latissimus dorsi, and triceps. With the hooking punch, the power is generated in a much different manner:

1) Centrifugal force is generated by sharply turning the waist.
2) Contraction of the deltoids and the pectorals, causing the arm to swing inward. 3) A controlling technique always augments the power of the punch.

Coordination of the waist and arm is critical to creating the whip-like effect which gives the hooking punch its power. Similar to the lifting punch, the practice of proper timing and coordination is the key. These can be trained alone in the air or against a target, as well as in actual sparring with a live opponent.

The Fighting Concept of Wing Tsun

Quite often the term "style" is used in reference to various forms of Chinese gongfu such as crane style, monkey style, hung style, dragon style etc., indicating that the techniques, behavior, and methods of a certain style fall into a recognizable aesthetic. Wing tsun as taught by Grandmaster Professor Leung Ting, being firmly rooted in pragmatism, can more accurately be described as a system rather than a style; more of a science than an art. For wing tsun is not just a collection of the favorite techniques of some long-dead martial arts patriarch; rather it is a system of inter-related fighting concepts to which certain techniques are applicable and from which others emerge.

Wing tsun's three punching methods work together as complimentary elements of a time-tested battle plan. For the wing tsun practitioner, the straight-line thrusting punch is the primary striking method; while the lifting punch and hooking punch are used as back up measures in situations where the straight punch is limited. The overall effectiveness of these techniques rests on the underlying strategy for their use. This is where the fighting concept of wing tsun comes in.

According to this concept, once a wing tsun practitioner is confronted by an attacker he will not hesitate; instead he will go immediately on the offensive as soon as the attacker comes within range. He will then pursue the attacker relentlessly until victory is achieved. There is no sizing up the opponent, no pausing, and no second guessing. It is simply an all or nothing approach. As explained by Grandmaster Professor Leung Ting, "If you fight, then no mercy. But if merciful, then don't fight." Practically speaking, this is the most efficient strategy that a smaller or weaker person can adopt when fighting a larger or stronger enemy. For if they cannot defeat their opponent quickly, then drawing the fight out over a longer period would be pointless. By taking the fight to the opponent, the wing tsun practitioner gains among other things, the element of surprise. In wing tsun terminology this is called "sticking to the enemy with pressing steps and punches" (*bik-bo-tip-da*).

Therefore, the attacker who targets a wing tsun practitioner will find himself up against an aggressive defender, whose initial response to being attacked is to counter-attack with a heavy barrage of chain punches aimed at their face and throat. It is worth noting that while the chain punches are thrown in quantity, they are not wasted. wing tsun does not advocate throwing any strike when out of range, and certainly not for the purpose of feigning.

As the wing tsun fighter is applying chain punches, the opponent is forced to either defend or be struck. If the chain punches land, they will be followed by even more chain punches, as well as knee and elbow strikes; continuing until the opponent is unable to respond. Should the punches fail to reach their intended target, any limb-to-limb contact made during this exchange will trigger the tactile reflexes developed by wing tsun's famous *chisau* (arm-clinging) exercise. This causes the wing tsun fighter to shift into even higher gear and begin trapping or by-passing the opponent's defenses in order to prosecute their attack. It is at this stage that the lifting punch and hooking punch arise; based on the type of resistance given by the opponent.

TECHNICAL SECTION

Process of Wing Tsun Chain Punching

Notice that the wrists will cross before the front hand is fully withdrawn from the front. The wing tsun chain punches seen from the side. First the rear hand begins thrusting forward (**A-1-2**). Next it crosses the wrist of the front hand (**A-3**); causing the front hand to drop down (**A-4**) making room for the completed punch (**A-5**). Finally the hand formerly in front will be totally withdrawn into ready position near the center of the chest (**A-6**).

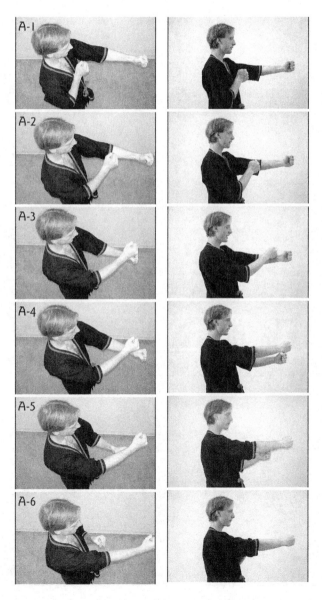

Advancing Step

Partner **A** poses the wing tsun pre-fighting posture and faces partner **B** (**B-1**). As **B** launches a reverse punch, **A** begins launching a wing tsun straight-line punch just prior to stepping forward (**B-2**). **A** uses the straight-line punch and his rear hand to check **B**'s punch, deflecting it while moving in (**B-3-4**). Finally, **A**'s punch lands heavily on **B**'s face (**B-5**) and would be followed with a barrage of chain punches.

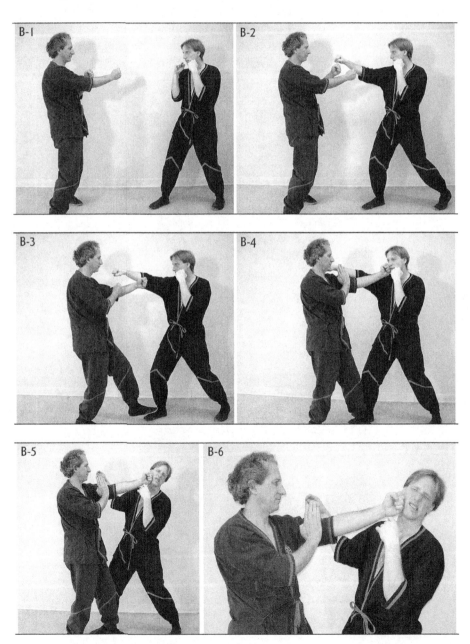

Lifting Punch sequence as seen in wing tsun's second empty-hand set known as "arm seeking" **(C-1-5)**. Beginning in the *bongsau* position **(C-1)**, the fist closes and elbow drops down slightly **(C-2)** as the body begins turning to the side **(C-3)**. Once turned, the fist thrusts upward and culminates in an upward lifting action of the spine **(C-4-5)**.

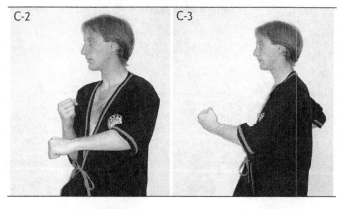

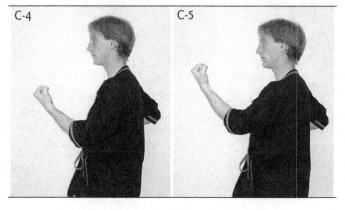

Lifting Punch Application

Neck pulling hand and lifting punch sequence: Partner **A** (left) confronts partner **B** (**D-1**), who initiates a punch to **A**'s face which it is intercepted by **A**'s lead arm (**D-2**). By using **B**'s on-coming force, **A** pulls him off balance and applies a neck pulling hand (**D-3-4**) which strikes heavily on the back of his neck, momentarily rendering him disoriented. **A** quickly launches the lifting punch at **B**'s throat (**D-5**) which strikes the larynx and crushes it (**D-6**).

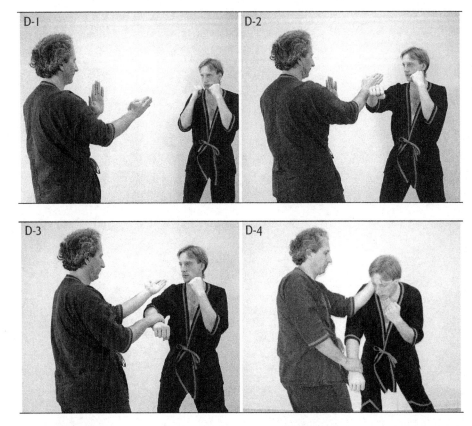

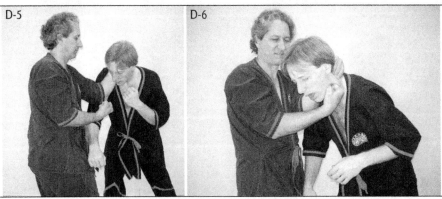

Hooking Punch Application

Partner **A** (left) approaches partner **B** and attacks him with a crossing reverse punch **(E-1-2)** which **B** intercepts with his lead arm. **B** uses the force of **A**'s punch to apply an arm lock which jerks him off balance **(E-3-4)** and throws him into a head-on collision with the wing tsun hooking punch **(E-5-7)**.

Hooking Punch Application

Partner **A** (left) throws a cross at partner **B** (**F-1-2**) which is intercepted with **B**'s lead arm. Making use of **A**'s force, **B** locks his arm and pulls him off balance (**F-3-4**). As **A** stumbles forward, **B** torques his waist and swings the arm (**F-5-6**) striking **A**'s throat with the full power of his body. **A** suffers a crushed windpipe (**F-7-8**) and cannot continue.

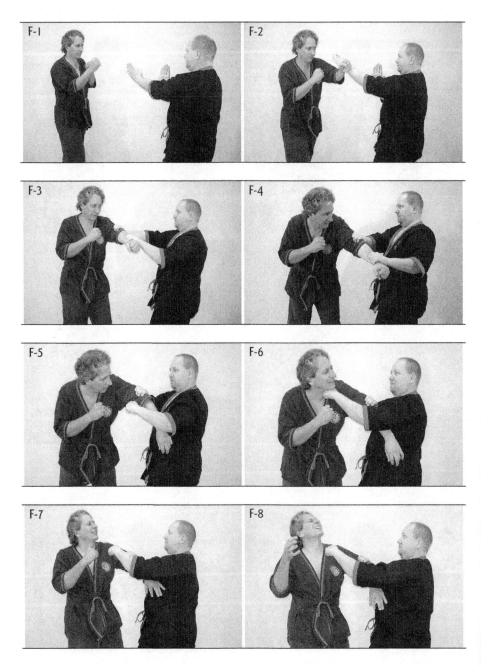

Hooking Punch Application

Partner **A** in a wing tsun frontal stance is confronted by **B** who throws a diagonal arm punch **(G-1-2)**. **A** grabs **B**'s wrist and due to the angle of **B**'s punch, cannot apply a straight-line punch, so he raises his elbow **(G-3)** and strikes with the hooking punch **(G-4)** to **B**'s temporomandibular joint **(G-5)**.

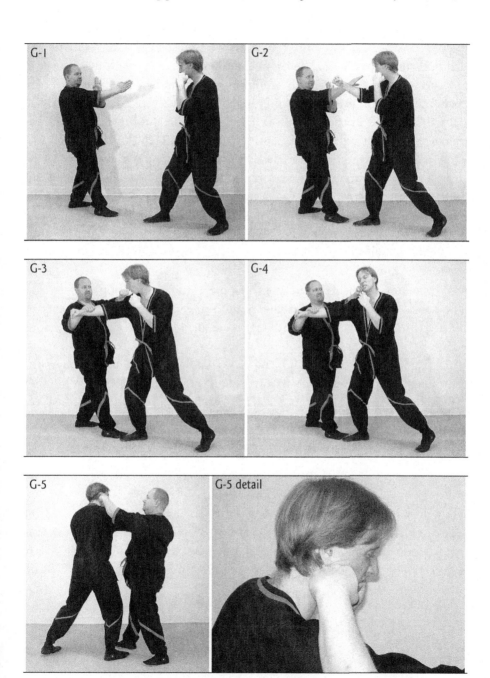

Conclusion

In summary, the three punches of wing tsun—namely the straight-line thrusting punch, the lifting punch, and the hooking punch—are among the most formidable and effective closed-fist strikes known. Each punch makes use of sound body-mechanics and delivers an impressive amount of striking power.

The straight-line thrusting punch, wing tsun's main offensive technique, is widely acknowledged for its effectiveness and therefore widely imitated. However, it is clear that this seemingly 'simple stroke' requires dedicated practice, sufficient physical development, and the correct fighting concept in order to reach its full potential. The lifting punch and hooking punch, which are commonly confused with similar punches in Western boxing, are in fact quite dissimilar with regard to how they are applied and the circumstances precipitating their use. Both the lifting and hooking punches arise when the wing tsun practitioner makes limb-to-limb contact while applying the straight-line thrusting punch, and the straight way is obstructed. Capitalizing on this contact, the wing tsun fighter will use a controlling technique either to pull the opponent into the next strike, or hold them in place in order to amplify the effects of the strike. Both the straight-line punch and lifting punch use similar muscle groups since each involves bringing the elbow inward prior to thrusting forward. In the case of the lifting punch, additional power is generated by an upward lifting motion of the spine at the culmination of the strike. The hooking punch, which visually shares some similarities with the boxing hook, utilizes distinctly different body-mechanics and methods of generating power.

Finally, we learned that it is the wing tsun fighting concept which unifies the three punches, wing tsun's footwork, and the tactile reflexes developed by the chisau exercise into a methodical and systematic approach to fighting.

Acknowledgment

The author would like to thank his teacher, Grandmaster Professor Leung Ting, for his patient instruction in both wing tsun and in his living philosophy. Great appreciation also to my students who appeared in the article—Dr. Larry Brown, Edward Flagg, and Jeremiah Robles, and also to Mr. Harry Lundell for his proof-reading.

CHINESE GLOSSARY

Cantonese *	Mandarin	Characters
au chong kuen	gou zhuang quan	勾撞拳
bik bo tip da	pobu tieda	迫步貼打
biutze	biaozhi	標指
chau chong kuen	chou zhuang quan	抽撞拳
chisau	chishou	黐手
chumkiu	xunqiao	尋橋
chin bo	zhan bu	戰步
lin wan chung kuen	lianhuan chong quan	連環衝拳
sil lim tao	xiao nian tou	小念頭
wing tsun kuen	yongchunquan	詠春拳
tat gee chung kuen	rizi chong quan	日字衝拳

Note: Romanization as used by Prof. Leung Ting

Bibliography

Hebb, D. (1949). *The organization of behavior*. New York: Wiley Publications.

Kernspecht, K. (1987). *Vom zweikampf*. [On single combat]. Burg/Fehmarn: Wu Shu Verlag Kernspecht.

Leung, T. (1985). *Dynamic wing tsun kungfu*. Hong Kong: Leung's Publications.

Leung, T. (1978). *Wing tsun kuen*. Hong Kong: Leung's Publications.

Tsatsouline, P. (2000). *Power to the people*. St. Paul: Dragon Door Publications.

chapter 3

Defending the Motherline: Wing Chun's Sil Lum Tao

by Joyotpaul Chaudhuri, Ph.D.

J. Chaudhuri in the first movement of the Sil Lim Tao routine.
Photo by Rob Day.

Wing chun (Cantonese, wing chun; Mandarin, yong chun) is a southern Chinese martial art that has been spreading in the British Commonwealth, the United States and parts of Continental Europe and Asia. We can thank the Chinese Revolution as a factor in this dispersion. The late Grandmaster Yip Man escaped to Hong Kong in 1950 and eventually began teaching publicly what was a fairly closed and disciplined tradition which veered off from southern Shaolin (Cantonese, Siu Lum) style over three centuries ago. The Bruce Lee phenomenon in movies and in the martial arts provided an additional early stimulation to the spreading of wing chun in America. Unfortunately, the spreading of wing chun was accompanied by considerable miscommunication and resulted in uneven quality control and a proliferation of hasty adaptations. Some of this confusion is understandable.

Yip Man, who died in 1972, was the major source of information on wing chun, yet his public teaching lasted less than fifteen years (1950-1964). He taught privately for several years afterwards.[1] Despite his profound understanding of wing chun, Yip Man was a reluctant teacher who did not directly or consistently correct all of his students. Hence, the beginning of the profusion of perceptions in the evolution of wing chun. Not all of the perceptions are of equal validity any more than a "C" student's lecture notes in an American university are as valid as those of an "A" student's even though both might "pass the course." Economic necessity drove Yip Man to teach; otherwise, as a man of property, he probably would have remained a leisurely patriarch practicing wing chun in *Fatshan* (Cantonese; Mandarin, *Foshan*) in southern China. The legacy that is left, however, is a deep, intriguing and virtually unexhaustible martial way of uniting body, mind and spirit.

Left to right: Joyotpaul Chaudhuri,
Ho Kam Ming, and Augustine Fong.
Photo courtesy of Charles Parker.

Discussing all aspects of wing chun is not possible in a book chapter. The author's focus here is to share a glimpse of the system through an analysis of the structure and function of the primary stance of wing chun in the first form, *sil lim tao* (Cantonese; Mandarin, *xiao nian tou*, "a little idea"), which instills the relational structure of bone, ligament, joint, tendon, muscle, line and angle, while also teaching the inner virtues of softness, stillness, sinking and emptiness. Hopefully, through this discussion the reader himself will understand the underlying logic of the subject, thereby minimizing a reliance on the statements of other authorities alone.

Now sixty-two years old, I have been interested and active in both Eastern and Western philosophy and martial arts for most of my life. For the last nineteen years, I have focused my studies on wing chun. My main teacher has been Augustine Fong, who is the most distinguished student of Ho Kam Ming, who, in turn, was one of the most distinguished students of Yip Man. Ho Kam Ming studied with Yip Man for over fifteen years and was personally very close to the Grandmaster until his death. With a background in comparative philosophy and martial arts, I questioned all aspects of wing chun's theory and practice. Some insightful answers came from related literature, Augustine Fong, and seminars with Ho Ham Ming, Wong Shun Leung, Chu Shong Tin, Victor Kan and others. I obtained additional information from visiting wing chun schools in the United States mainland, Hawaii, and Hong Kong. Thus, I obtained many perspectives on the art. However, despite these authoritative sources, much is based on common sense regarding the subject.

A Martial Way

The structure of wing chun as a way to truth uses the practice of self-defense as a search for wisdom.[2] The conquest of fear is part of the journey of liberation and understanding the Self is a key to its defense. As in the Dhyana-Chan-Zen Buddhist perspectives in the arts, one progresses through various spiritual stages, e.g., through *samsara*, nirvana and then to the Void. In the martial wing chun way, one conquers the delusions and misperceptions and then sees the problematic situation as it really is before one begins to understand the Void. Of course, as in many Chinese contexts, the Chan perspective may have an overlay of Daoist nomenclature as well (such as the Five Element Theory) or a Confucian schooling structure for martial arts study, such as master-student or elder-brother/younger-brother relationships. But the Dhyana-Chan-Zen perspective is a sufficient guide for understanding the principles of wing chun.

Sil Lim Tao: The Roots of Wing Chun

Many of the principles of wing chun come together in the primary stance of the sil lim tao form. The stance includes a complex of geometrical shapes, including interrelated triangles, circles and lines. Externally, they form a stable pyramid-like structure with broad triangles visible from the front, the back, or the sides. The center of gravity is not as low or as wide as in some horse-riding stances nor as narrow and high as in Western boxing. The feet are sufficiently pigeon-toed to form a base triangle and the turned-in knees point toward the apex of the base triangle. There are other horizontal triangles at the hips and the elbows. There are vertical triangles from the shoulders toward the heart, the *dantian*, and the middle-line between the knees. This last elongated, vertical, downward-pointing triangle meets the upward-pointing, shorter but broader

40

triangle coming from the feet. The two triangles meet at the knees. The coordinated turns, initiated at the knees, control the motion of both the base triangle and the longer, inverted triangle from the shoulders down. The torque around the center-line by the base delivers tremendous energy to the top so that the hands can move quickly. The base is strong but potentially very mobile while the top can turn and spring faster, thereby providing fluid power and multiple, nearly simultaneous actions. Hence, the traditional designation: "Feet like a mountain; hands like lightning."

With the tailbone tucked in with a pelvic tilt, the sacral area is rooted like a shovel stuck into the ground at a slight angle. The middle part of the back rests straight while the upper back tilts slightly forward. The head and neck are straight with the chin tucked in. This makes for a functionally straight spine so energy can flow evenly along its pathway. The feeling is that of hanging from a string while being rooted to the ground.

The entire structural pyramid has several lines which are the key to the mobility of the wing chun structure. The most important line is called the "motherline," which is the axis from the apex straight down through the middle of the pyramid to the ground between the legs. The motherline acts like a pivotal rod or axis and every fluid motion involves a visible or imperceptible turn of the motherline. In the first form, since the feet remain stationary, the motherline does not shift sideways or back and forth. However, even though the lower body is stationary in the sil lim tao, the sensitive student becomes aware that there is a lot of internal movement in the first form. While the motherline is vertically straight and stable, the punches, palm strikes and other movements all emanate from the motherline, which create various lines going out like spokes from the hub of a wheel. And everything is interrelated.

When the left hand moves, there is a compensatory balancing move on the right side because of the circular action of the central axis, or motherline. The entire person is essentially a bundle of energy formed around an axis, with the dantian below the navel being the center of the bundle. A wise martial artist simply protects his or her motherline, conserves energy at the center and attacks or controls the motherline of the other person.

All of the triangles, lines, circles, and geometric shapes are connected to the motherline. The vertical motherline has a series of connecting points which serve as axes for horizontal lines and planes. One axis is at the heart and another one is in the pelvic area. These two horizontal lines cross the motherline creating six so-called "gates." The two top gates above the heart are protected by the hands. The two middle gates can be protected by the hands or the legs. The two bottom gates are protected by the feet alone (see page 38). There are additional lines and planes located at the dantian, shoulders, elbows, hips and knees. Awareness of the lines and the axes and being able to turn them without breaking the structure creates a very mobile and flexible system. The structure is effective when standing, moving forwards, backwards, sideways, sitting, bending, or lying down. But learning how to stand and understand the mother-line is the prelude to all motion. Hence, the importance of the first form—*sil lim tao* (Mandarin, *xiao nian tou*)—"a little idea" of an extensive system.

Like all art, there is an element of both science and physics involved. But in Asian arts, there are also aspects of the esoteric, intuitive, aesthetic and denotative components and meanings in the proper uses of the wing chun structure. The whole is greater than the sum of its parts. Hence, as in other Asian arts, a knowledgeable guide or teacher is important, particularly in the beginning of the journey, which includes understanding of the motherline.

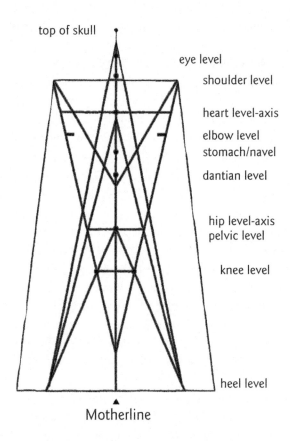

The Motherline

The Motherline: A Comparative View

Understanding the motherline and all her horizontal and vertical children coming out of the axis is fundamental to learning wing chun. There are unlimited possibilities of combinations and techniques. But adapting and modifying wing chun techniques without understanding the principles limits the character and usefulness of imitated techniques.

Brief comparisons of the structure of wing chun with other, better known systems should help in understanding the nature of the legacy of wing chun. Among taijiquan styles, for example, the Chen Style is the oldest. Like wing chun, Chen taiji can be approached from a variety of perspectives for learning, i.e., self-defense, health, art, philosophy, and wisdom. Chen style has an explosive compactness. Learning the two traditional forms leads to a comprehensive set of applications. In addition to striking techniques made with the hands, elbows and feet, the Chen style includes blocks, controlling motions, and throws flowing from movements following circular and linear patterns.[3]

A major source of the great moving energy in the Chen style comes from uncoiling, spiralling-upward movements with the waist playing a major role. When applied to push-hands routines, this energy manifests in circular motions similar to hula-hoop gyrations. There are, however, small side-to-side motions, which result in the swaying of the motherline. In wing chun, while the motherline remains sufficiently supple, it does not sway; it revolves on its axis, creating a drilling, rifle-like motion.

In many other martial arts, various parts of the motherline are used from the hip up or the waist up. This appears to be the case for boxing, judo and karate. In contrast, awareness of the entire motherline and flexible stability is emphasized in the sil lim tao. Later the student learns how to turn, step, move and use the horizontal lines and the connecting axes in the second and third forms of wing chun.

The pre-eminence of the motherline in wing chun is also seen in training with a wooden dummy as well as with weapons. While one works with the arms and legs of the wooden dummy, the real focus is on the motherline of the dummy's trunk. The arms and legs and the slats have some give, but basically the dummy's trunk and motherline are stable. This practice trains one's movements to search for the dummy's motherline without destabilizing one's own motherline. Not understanding this, improperly trained enthusiasts indiscriminately beat on the dummy's arms and legs rather than learning the relationships between the lines represented in the motherline theory.

Then there are martial art styles in which practitioners collapse their motherlines by acrobatic flying leaps, jumps, and spins, often with kicks resulting from these motions. Wing chun has lots of kicks, but they are applied without destabilizing the motherline. Often, wing chun kicks occur when one has some control of the opponent through touch so that contact with the opponent's structure is maintained. There are some small hopping motions in wing chun, but they are intended to regain control of the line, i.e., the relationship between one's motherline and the opponent's. The orientation toward the integrity of the motherline and its axis is a singular characteristic of the art of wing chun.

Motion in the Sil Lim Tao

Once the structure and function of the stance in sil lim tao is understood, a brief overview of the hand motions is in order. While the stance is being learned and strengthened, the hand motions provide an introduction to both internal and external principles. The first movement involving "palm up," "defensive hand," and "twisted hand" are done very, very slowly so that the mind understands the right amount of energy to use, the movement on the correct line, and the even control of energy flow. At the same time, the importance of the elbow, its drilling motion and its control of the line is developed.

After the first slow sections, the remainder of the 108 movements are done at a more rapid but controlled pace. However, the elegance and simplicity of the system can be seen from the fact that all the hand motions of wing chun are derived from three basic hand motions—"palm up," "defensive hand," and "twisted hand"—and these three motions, in turn, involve three stages of circular, forward and drilling motions around the chest-level axis, directed by the elbows.

Left: J. Chaudhuri practicing with a wooden dummy in his studio. *Photo courtesy of John Kowal.* Right: blocking and cutting with "eight way chopping knives." *Photo courtesy of Rob Day.*

Chisao

The three hand motions are the elements of chisao—the unique "sticky-hand" motion of wing chun, which develops endless skills, including timing, appropriate power and reflexes, sensitivity, knowledge of the lines, structure, weaknesses, and strengths. Chisao develops sensors which provide a wealth of information immediately upon contact. Chisao has many varieties: several single "sticky-hand" motions and several double "sticky-hand" motions. In turn, "sticky-hand" can be done in different contexts: standing, sitting, moving, blindfolded, and with or without various single-leg, double-leg, and "sticky-leg" motions. All these chisao motions can flow into each other and also flow into "grabbing arm" motions. In turn, the chisao motions can provide the occasion for experimenting with families or formations involving different openings and endings and defenses against them. And chisao can be done with a rich variety of wing chun footwork.

Chisao's drilling (not up and down) motions are different from the more side-to-side motions of taiji's push-hands exercises. Chisao is sometimes imitated by modified or "eclectic" systems. But there cannot be good chisao without understanding wing chun and there cannot be good wing chun without chisao. The theory and the practice go together in the development of the applications and the evolution of individuality and spontaneity.

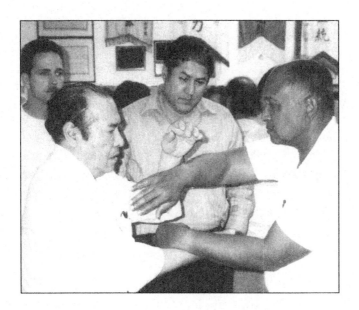

Ho Kam Ming correcting the author's chisao motions.
Photo courtesy of Charles Parker.

With learning the sil lim tao, how to turn and step, and then developing the sensitivity of chisao, the wing chun student is well on the way to effective self-defense. However, a word of caution is in order. People with actual fighting experience have some basic initial advantages. But compensating with lots of chisao is the appropriate long-run training remedy. The learning curve of only fighting can be steep but short, declining with injury and age. In contrast, the wing chun learning curve, because of chisao, continues steadily upward. Yip Man remained formidable until his last illness and Ho Kam Ming remains formidable in his seventies. The key is chisao—for which one should always be prepared to learn something new every time it is practiced.

SOME KEY APPLICATIONS AND GUIDELINES

A brief discussion of applications follows regarding the structure, function, motions, and principles of wing chun and the practice of chisao. There are endless possible applications, since there are many permutations and combinations that can occur between different people in different places and situations. But some select examples of operational principles will hopefully illustrate the practical results of the theory of the lab work.

- **Motherline**
  Always protect your own motherline. If the gates to the motherline are closed, the opponent has to take circuitous routes, leaving the wing chun person to effectively control shorter, more direct lines to the opponent.

- **Center**
  The ultimate target is the opponent's motherline. Destroying the motherline will cut off the necessary energy links of potential techniques.

- **Inside Line**
  In every situation, if at all possible, capture the inside line. Doing so neutralizes the opponent's speed and power. For example, if the opponent throws a straight jab at the face, a rising straight punch between the jab and the path or connection between the opponent and your own motherline captures or wins the inside line. This is truly an intercepting fist when it can be a block which continues into an attack.

- **Kicking**
  Kick only when your structure is stable due to proper balance or due to borrowing your opponent's structure by controlling the contact point, i.e., by grabbing, blocking, touching, or even hitting. Then the kicks can be "invisible" or "shadowless," i.e., cannot be seen by the opponent unless he foolishly looks down and thereby gets into greater difficulties.

- **Force Relations**
  If the attacking force is weak and you have the inside line, then attack. If the attacking force is close to parity, deflect with a turn while attacking. If the

opposite force is stronger than yours and you have to defend yourself by fighting, use one of the wing chun sidesteps and turn and attack. Also, when stopping a stronger force at close quarters, the right amount of giving and softness will prevent a breakdown of your own structure. The same principle applies when spring-nets and lines on the decks of U.S. Navy aircraft carriers stop a landing plane in a short distance.

- **Combinations**
When your structure is sound, you can launch multiple attacks with one motion of the structure. A very short step or turn can launch both hands and a leg—if the balance is right.

- **Trapping**
Wing chun is known for its trapping. But imitations of wing chun often do not go beyond trapping with hands. With progressive chisao there is far more to trapping. With the development of the feet, the martial artist learns how to go beyond the hands to the trapping of the motion, the energy, the stance, the structure, and ultimately, the intentions or emotions of the opponent. And if the opponent's emotions are successfully directed away from the developing conflict, then indeed one has won without fighting—the ultimate victory.

Wing Chun Techniques Illustrating
the Importance of the Motherline
Photos by Rob Day.

A-1: As an attacker (Terry Nowicki) approaches, Mr. Chaudhuri takes a defensive position.

A-2: Chaudhuri blocks Nowicki's punch while attacking the neck with a palm-up, spade-hand strike. **A-3:** The defensive hand becomes an attacking "pressing palm" to the opponent's chin, while the other hand grabs the opponent's shoulder. **A-4:** Changing the palms to apply pressure to the top and bottom axis points of the center line destabilizes the attacker. **A-5:** The attacker falls towards the ground as directed by Chaudhuri's left hand while the right hand strikes the kidney area with the palm.

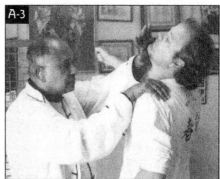

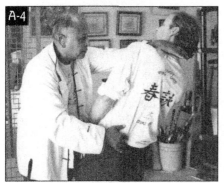

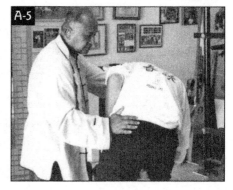

B-1: Mr. Nowicki begins an overhead strike with an escrima stick. **B-2:** Chaudhuri blocks the stick with a "throw away hand."

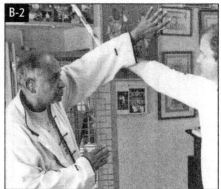

B-3: A double-slapping hand destabilizes the attacker. **B-4:** Chaudhuri's left hand contributes to the attacker's fall while his right hand attacks the groin.

C-1: An attacker approaches. **C-2:** As the attacker steps closer to punch, Chaudhuri pivots and blocks with his left hand.

C-3: The left hand circles downward and continues to divert the opponent's arm to the outside. Chaudhuri simultaneously strikes at the opponent's middle section with a spade hand while his right palm strikes at the opponent's jaw. **C-4:** The right hand grabs the opponent's neck while the left hand controls his body and then breaks the opponent's shoulder with the resulting leverage. **C-5:** Chaudhuri's left hand continues its circling motion to throw the opponent down. Note how Chaudhuri's left knee presses against the opponent's knee to further weaken the structure.

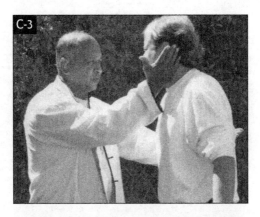

The author and his teacher, Augustine Fong, commencing with double "sticky hand." *Photo courtesy of Charles Parker.*

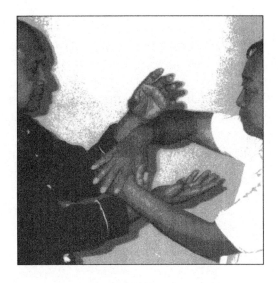

J. Chaudhuri applies a technique often practiced with a wooden dummy to counter an attack by Percy Naoroji. Note how the attacker's structure is trapped in addition to his being blocked and attacked. *Photo courtesy of John Kowal.*

Conclusion

We have given some applications of wing chun in self-defense situations. These include protecting the motherline, attacking the opponent's motherline, capturing the inside line, multiple action or combinations and finally, trapping. These applications emerge from the theories of wing chun and the laboratory of chisao. The major path to knowledge in the wing chun system is in the form of the sil lim tao— "the little idea."

It is possible to be like Miyamoto Mushashi, to gain wisdom through reflection, meditation, and the study of martial arts. But Mushashi himself was a guide and in great disciplines like wing chun it is better to have a guide. While great art has a foundation in denotative science shared with other arts, it is also full of connotative and esoteric meanings. Wing chun has both its science and its art. The sil lim tao binds the rings of earth, water, fire and wind with the void in a profound way.[4]

Notes

[1] See Yip Man's notes on "The Origin of Ving Tsun," pages 8-10 and Lok Yiu's essay, "Development of Ving Tsun Kung Fu in Hong Kong," pages 12-20 in *The genealogy of the wing tsun family* (1990). Hong Kong: Ving Tsun Athletic Association.

[2] For an excellent treatise on the relationship between martial activity and wisdom, see Nagaboshi, T. (1994), *The bodhisattva warriors*. York Beach, Maine: Samuel Weiser, Inc. For a source book on wing chun theory, see Fong, A. (n.d.). The complete systems of wing chun gung fu: Wing chun theories and concepts vol. 7. Tucson: Fong's Health Center. Also, see Fong, A. (n.d.). *Wing chun kung fu: History, concepts and philosophy*, Video No. 8. San Clemente, CA: Panther Productions.

For a discussion of the conceptual linkages between India and China in the martial arts, see Chaudhuri, J. (January, 1991). "108 step: The Sino-Indian connection in the martial arts." *Inside Kung Fu*, pp. 48-49 and 81-82.

[3] The author was introduced to Chen Style taijiquan by Jin Hengli, a national wushu champion from China. Additional corrections to the author's practice were made by Chen Xiaowang during his first trip to Phoenix and Tucson, Arizona.

[4] See Kaufman, S. (1994), *The martial artist's book of five rings*. Boston: Charles E. Tuttle Co. Within the circle of extant martial art systems, Mushashi's esoteric teachings appear to have considerable congruence with wing chun principles.

chapter 4

A Study in Maximizing Speed through Ving Tsun Concepts

by Jeff Webb

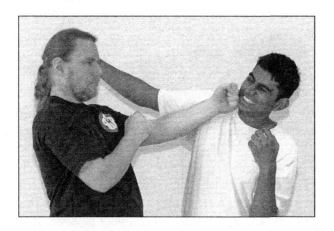

Illustrations courtesy of Jeff Webb.

A Study in Maximizing Speed through Ving Tsun Concepts

As human beings, most of what we learn about speed comes from everyday experiences. Getting up late means needing to rush in order to get to work on time. Cooking something too fast generally results in a ruined meal. Driving into an intersection while someone else is trying to beat the red light can literally be a life-altering experience. Generally speaking, our associations with speed are linked to the dire consequences of having either too much of it or simply not enough. Likewise, developing speed in our martial arts training can be considered one of the most important goals, along with the development of strength or power. How often in training have we attempted to block, strike, or move faster than our opponent? How often has not doing so given our opponent the upper hand? Speed is indeed crucial to success in the martial arts. Yet what is it that allows one person to move more quickly than another? *Webster's* defines speed as (a) the act or state of moving swiftly; and (b) rate of motion (Merriam-Webster, 2011). But these are rather generic definitions for a much more sophisticated subject. As applied to the martial arts, speed is much more than sheer physical velocity. In fact, it can be subdivided into two distinct categories: actual speed and relative speed.

Actual Speed vs. Relative Speed

Actual speed is defined as the true physical speed at which a martial artist is able to move. Whether it be a punch, a kick, or techniques that involve moving the whole body, this is the measureable rate at which a physical movement occurs. As an athlete, the trained martial artist possesses a greater capacity for actual speed than the lay person, due to physical conditioning and training. However, even the trained expert is limited by two factors, namely physics and genetics. Natural laws of motion as well as the limitations of the human body place a ceiling on just how fast one can physically move. Therefore, once the human potential for actual speed has been reached, it is only through the application of relative speed that one may seem to move even faster. Relative speed can be defined as the rate of motion one object exhibits in relation to another. This concept, though a bit more abstract, can be illustrated by two hypothetical travelers leaving Dallas for Boston by airplane. Traveler **A** boards a plane in Dallas on a direct flight to Boston. At the same instant, traveler **B** also boards a flight in Dallas that is Boston bound but has a connection in Chicago en route. Both traveler **A** and **B** have the same origin and destination, but traveler **A** will arrive first by taking a shorter route. Essentially, actual speed can be looked upon as relying purely upon physical effort to move quickly, whereas relative speed seeks to move more efficiently and with different (i.e., better) timing than the opponent. While both actual and relative speeds are important in the martial arts, those who always seem to be one step ahead of their opponents are typically those persons best able to combine the two.

Physical Basis of Actual Speed

The ability to move at a high rate of speed is a function of two factors: muscular conditioning and the maintenance of a relaxed overall musculature. Muscular conditioning is achieved by repeating a particular movement over and over until it becomes well coordinated. Later the practitioner will perform the same movement with effort applied toward increasing the rate of speed. Depending on the type of movement, different forms of resistance can also be incorporated into the training. The result will be muscles that are stronger, denser, capable of contracting more forcefully, and able to put the body into motion more rapidly.

At this point it is important to discuss the concept of slow-twitch and fast-twitch muscle fibers. Slow-twitch fibers are those that take approximately 80–100 milliseconds to achieve maximum isometric tension and that do not easily tire. Fast-twitch fibers, on the other hand, reach maximum isometric tension in about 40–60 milliseconds and, once stimulated, tend to fatigue rather quickly (Hamilton and Luttgens, 2002). It is worth stating that there are no fast-twitch muscles, merely fast-twitch muscle fibers. The muscles of the body contain both fast- and slow-twitch fibers, though in varying proportions. For example, the muscles of the arms and legs each possess roughly equal numbers of both types of fibers. Also, while the number of muscle fibers themselves cannot be increased, the quantity of myofibrils (i.e., the contractile units within each muscle fiber) can be increased. As with any physical activity, it is a common experience that the ease of performing a given motion increases proportionally to the cumulative number of repetitions performed. Initially, a great deal of this can be attributed to the strengthening of individual muscles. Once a beginner starts training, he or she will naturally begin to notice gains in strength and consequently in speed. Yet research has shown that after a period of time, further gains in strength (and speed) come less from muscular conditioning and more from intermuscular coordination (Kieser, 2003). At a certain point, muscular conditioning reaches a plateau as the body intuitively seeks to improve coordination between the muscle groups.

It is at this phase where targeted relaxation training can improve actual speed. Relaxation training in Ving Tsun gongfu is crucial to achieving the highest rates of sheer physical speed. The ability of individual muscles to contract quickly and forcefully is greatly enhanced when they can do so independently of their antagonist counterparts. Therefore, the goal in Ving Tsun is to maintain a general state of suppleness in the muscles and to contract only those muscles needed for a specific task, without affecting the other muscles of the body.

Ving Tsun gongfu belongs to the category of martial arts that has been best described as soft, internal, or, more accurately, flexible. This is in contrast to styles such as traditional karate or hard-style gongfu, which can be described as hard, external, or rigid. Since Ving Tsun focuses on cultivating this flexible force (yao), the initial training emphasizes targeted muscle relaxation and control. The first phase begins with the sil lim tao (little idea) practice routine in which relaxed body movement is the main goal. Unnecessary muscular tension is avoided and the techniques are initially performed so softly as to seem lacking in martial application. In fact, learning to avoid the use of brute force (gong) is so counterintuitive that many students initially find the concept hard to grasp. Perhaps the most eloquent explanation of this comes from another soft style, taijiquan, and the words of the venerable Zheng Manqing (Cheng Man-ch'ing). In T'ai-Chi: The "Supreme Ultimate" Exercise for Health, Sport, and Self-Defense (1967: 110), coauthor Robert W. Smith asks Master Zheng:

> In most fighting arts, students have invariably approached and surpassed the achievements of their teachers. Why is it that none of your pupils approach you? Indeed, irrespective of how rapidly some have progressed, all of them fall far below your level. What is the secret?

Zheng Manqing replies (1967: 101),

> You are right [sic] there is a secret. But it is so simple as to be unbelievable.
> Its nature insists that you believe, that you have faith; otherwise you will
> fail. The secret is simply this: you must relax your body and mind totally.
> You must be prepared to accept defeat repeatedly and for a long period;
> you must "invest in loss"—otherwise you will never succeed. I succeeded
> to my present state because I pushed pride aside and believed my master's
> words . . . Gradually my technique improved. Then and then only, did my
> responses sharpen so that neutralizing and countering were the work of a
> moment. My students either do not believe in this path or, if they do, they
> do not pursue it eagerly enough.

The focused relaxation described by Zheng and also practiced in Ving
Tsun gongfu has a kinesiological basis as well. In the process of muscular
contraction there exists a law known as the force-velocity relationship. It states
that, "the velocity of contraction is maximal when the load is zero, and the load
is maximal when the velocity is zero" (Hamilton & Luttgens, 2002). In layman's
terms, the absence of a load (i.e., tension) enables a muscle to contract at its
maximum speed. This would indicate that the more relaxed a muscle is, the
greater its potential for rapid contraction and therefore faster execution of a
martial arts technique. To summarize, actual speed is the ability to put the body
into motion at high velocity, which is dependent on sufficient conditioning of
the muscles and an ability to maintain relaxation in those muscles until they
are put into use. Furthermore, the rate at which a muscle relaxes after use directly
affects its ability to contract rapidly during subsequent techniques.

Relative Speed: The Focus of Ving Tsun Theory

Earlier in this chapter, relative speed was described simply as the rate of
motion, that one object exhibits in relation to another. Those familiar with
Ving Tsun gongfu most often associate it with aspects related to actual speed,
such as rapid-fire chain punches and quick, shuffling steps. Paradoxically, the
traditional theories of Ving Tsun gongfu say little about the development
of actual speed and focus primarily on the application of superior relative
speed.

The *kuen kuit* (boxing mnemonic) is a list of Ving Tsun gongfu mottos,
axioms, and theories that have been handed down since ancient times.
They encompass a wide range of key points dealing with proper execution
of techniques, fighting strategies, and the philosophies behind the system.
For the purposes of this chapter, I have selected five Ving Tsun mottos that best
illustrate the concept of relative speed.

MOTTO 1: "Simultaneous Attack and Defense"

"Simultaneous attack and defense" is undoubtedly the most famous of all Ving Tsun axioms. By simultaneous, we mean that the defensive technique occurs at the same or nearly the same instant as the counterattacking technique. This is in stark contrast to most styles, where block and counter are performed as two separate actions. Typically this is done so that full power can be committed to the blocking technique. Since Ving Tsun defenses are based on borrowing the opponent's force rather than clashing with it, using full power when defending is unnecessary. Occasionally one finds mention of simultaneous attack and defense in other styles, though the accuracy of this description is questionable. The book *Dynamic Karate* by M. Nakayama lists six distinct possibilities when blocking, one of which reads, "block and attack. Block the opponent's attack and immediately counterattack. It is also possible to block and counterattack at the same instant" (Nakayama, 1966). On the surface this may seem analogous to the concept of "simultaneous attack and defense," yet the examples given typically involve striking the attacker collaterally with the blocking arm as it is being swung. The correct interpretation of "simultaneous attack and defense" takes into account that both arms—and often one of the legs—should be used simultaneously. In the case of defending a lower punch, the *gedan barai* of karate is a two-step movement. First the lower block is performed and, afterward, the counterattack is launched. Ving Tsun's answer is a one-step movement called *gaun-da*, which is a lower defense applied in coordination with a simultaneous punch. By performing the defense and counter in one step, it is accurate to say that this Ving Tsun technique is literally twice as fast as its karate counterpart.

Examples of Simultaneous Attack and Defense

A) Conventional block and counter: Partner *A* steps forward and launches a low punch. *B* defends with a low block followed by a reverse punch.

B) Simultaneous Ving Tsun defense using both hands: *A* steps forward and launches a low punch. *B* defends with a ploughing hand block (*gaun da*) and straight-line thrusting punch.

C) Simultaneous Ving Tsun defense using hand and foot: *A* attacks with a straight punch, which *B* defends with a hacking hand strike (*pak sau*) and lower thrust kick.

MOTTO 2: *"Attacking Hand is Defending Hand"*

Nakayama's aforementioned example of block and counterattack in the same instant is clearly not the same as "simultaneous attack and defense," but more closely resembles another Ving Tsun theory: "Attacking hand is defending hand." Yet upon closer inspection, it could even be said that the Ving Tsun interpretation of this concept is antithetical to Nakayama's, based on his given examples. The Ving Tsun application is to attack in a manner that also counter-defends, whereas Nakayama advocates blocking in a manner that also counter-attacks. Lest this sound like splitting hairs, this difference is an important one. Blocking is a defensive action taken subsequent to an attack and therefore subject to timing complications described by Nakayama himself: "Defense against an attack in karate is a more complicated process than it appears at first glance. To begin with, you must anticipate the nature and direction of your opponent's attack before blocking it" (Nakayama, 1966). Keith Kernspecht, the noted European Ving Tsun expert, also discussed this dilemma in *On Single Combat* (1987), where he clearly described the total time required to defend as the sum of reaction time (i.e., anticipation and block selection) plus blocking time (i.e., the length of time it takes to perform the block).

While the time required to perform a block is not the key issue, Nakayama would probably agree that the time involved in anticipating and then selecting an appropriate block certainly is. *Da sau jik siu sau* means counterattacking in response to an attack, using the angle of our own attack as defense against the attack of the enemy. Most often this is accomplished by wedging and deflecting the enemy's attack while that of the Ving Tsun practitioner remains on course. At the basic levels of Ving Tsun this is accomplished with the hands, and at the advanced levels the same is done with kicks.

Examples of Attacking Hand is Defending Hand

A) Example of Nakayama's upper block: Partner *A* advances with a reverse punch. *B* counters with an upward block from beneath the attacker's arm, which strikes collaterally to face.

B) Example of Ving Tsun attack that also defends: Partner *A* punches to *B's* face. *B* counter-attacks with a straight-line thrusting punch, wedging out *A's* punch and striking him in the face.

MOTTO 3: "Start Last, Finish First"

One might well question the chances of winning a race when getting off to a late start. Truly this can be a handicap, but how often in our daily lives do we get a late start on something yet finish before our competitors? Imagine two students given a writing assignment. One might start writing immediately but make relatively slow progress, while his counterpart, getting a later start, works feverishly and finishes way ahead of him. The Ving Tsun concept of "start last, finish first" can be illustrated by the use of a frontal thrust kick to counter a roundhouse or spinning kick. Once the attacker has initiated the roundhouse kick, the defender must quickly launch a linear counterkick, relying on the shorter and quicker movement as a defense. While there is certainly nothing wrong with using circular movements, properly timed linear movements can often beat the opponent to the punch.

By countering a circular kick with a linear kick aimed at the torso, the kicking leg, or even the standing leg, there is the added benefit of simultaneously disrupting the attacker's balance. Whenever possible, the Ving Tsun practitioner will attempt to exploit the enemy's balance, effectively robbing him of the ability to use his power. Through the use of specialized footwork, it is also possible to counter a linear kicking technique by stepping forward in a circular fashion and striking with the hands. This tactic conforms to both "start last, finish first" and another Ving Tsun axiom: "punch the head, no kicks" (*da tau mo gerk*). Any technique conforming to the "start last, finish first" concept will be initiated closely after the opponent launches an attack and will be performed at top physical speed. As we have seen in the two examples above, the "start last, finish first" concept is not a choice between linear or circular; it is about which timing works best in each situation.

Examples of Start Last, Finish First

A) A straight line is faster: Partner *A* attacks with a roundhouse kick. *B*, though starting later, uses a frontal thrust kick to counterattack.

B) Circling is faster: Partner *A* attacks with a front snap kick. *B* begins his circular advancing step after partner *A* is already in motion, countering with a punch to the head.

MOTTO 4: "One-Point Attack"

It is said that mathematics is the most common language on planet earth. In the real world, one plus one always equals two, regardless of whether you are in the USA, Germany, or Hong Kong. This also applies to a sequence of movements. Given two combatants possessing equal rates of actual physical speed, a technique that consists of a single motion will always be faster than a chain of two or more techniques. As we discussed in the previous section on *hau fat sin ji*, it is indeed possible to start last and finish first. What isn't possible is linking two, three, or more techniques together in a lengthy sequence and expecting they could be applied much faster than a single technique. As a Ving Tsun national instructor, I often encounter martial artists who have learned a handful of Ving Tsun moves from somewhere, and upon which they claim a comprehensive knowledge of the entire system. What many people fail to understand about Ving Tsun is that the techniques are not as important as the concepts behind them. A case in point is an instructor I met who specialized in a popular adrenal-stress training method, as well as in taekwondo. By attempting to demonstrate the speed of a three-step Ving Tsun technique he had learned somewhere, he was unable to grasp the logic that the one-step technique I showed him was indeed faster. "You don't understand," he said. "This combination is really fast. It's all about the speed you're building up when you do it." My reply was, "Yes, those moves are fast, but the three of them in series simply aren't faster than my one movement." After giving him a practical demonstration several times, he eventually, albeit begrudgingly, conceded the point. True Ving Tsun seeks to use the fewest movements to achieve its goals, and never uses multiple defensive movements back to back before launching a counterattack. Counterattacks are critical in convincing an attacker to cease and desist. By only defending, one invites continued attacks.

Examples of One-Point Attack

A) Often confused as legitimate Ving Tsun, the wing arm (*bongsau*) to slapping hand (*lapsau*), to backfist maneuver partner *A* attacks partner *B's* lead arm.

B) The legitimate Ving Tsun technique is the hacking hand strike (*pat da*), a one-point attack, which *A* uses against *B's* lead arm.

C) Another not-so-correct Ving Tsun sequence: Partner *A* attacks with a low punch. *B* steps back with a *gaunsau*, followed by a *gumsau* and a backfist.

D) The legitimate Ving Tsun defense is the pinning hand strike (*gum da*), a one-point technique. As *A* attempts the low punch, *B* counters at once with a compound attack and defense.

MOTTO 5: "Enemy Doesn't Move, I Don't Move; Enemy Moves Once, I Move First"

This final motto has as much to do with relative speed as with the proper attitude of a Ving Tsun fighter. When approached, the Ving Tsun practitioner should always be ready, poised, and looking for the first hint of movement from the opponent that signals his need to act. Typically, a combatant is most vulnerable once he has begun executing a technique and is in midmotion. Whether that movement is a position change, a feint, or an actual attack is inconsequential. Attacking the opponent quickly, just as he begins to move, dramatically disrupts his timing.

Naturally, when discussing this concept, the topic of feints must be addressed. Indeed, some arts, such as boxing, effectively use feints to trigger a reaction from the opponent, thereby setting up a subsequent attack. Feinting is advantageous when the intended victim subscribes to a block-then-counter defensive method. Fortunately the first concept we mentioned, "simultaneous attack and defense," already takes this into account and reveals feints as the shadows they truly are. A properly trained Ving Tsun expert cannot be tricked into defending, but can certainly be provoked into launching an aggressive counterattack that is simultaneously accompanied by defensive measures.

A feint against a Ving Tsun fighter, then, is essentially a wasted opportunity to have actually attacked. As with any effective, functional system, Ving Tsun has numerous built-in redundancies and overlapping safeguards. Dovetailing perfectly with this Ving Tsun principle is another that states *jiu ying but jiu sau*, or, "Chase the body posture; don't chase the hands." Interpreted, this means the Ving Tsun fighter is not concerned with chasing the opponent's limbs; rather his goal is to attack the body (i.e., head, neck, and torso). The chasing of hands only takes the problem of reaction time, which was previously mentioned, and compounds it. When feinted, the defender does him- or herself no favors by merely holding ground and blocking, or even by retreating and blocking. Under those conditions, the effectiveness of either a single feint or progressive feints is undeniable.

But consider instead an opponent who will respond to a feint by moving quickly and aggressively into close range, with kamikaze-like abandon, and who is focused fully on destroying the attacker with a barrage of rapid, full-power strikes to the head and throat. This is the aggressive attitude of preemption embodied in the concept of "Enemy doesn't move, I don't move; enemy moves once, I move first."

Examples of Enemy Doesn't Move, I Don't Move; Enemy Moves Once, I Move First
A) Partner *A* falls victim to *B* when a feinted low roundhouse kick changes quickly to high roundhouse kick.

B) The Ving Tsun solution is planned: attack the moment the enemy moves. When partner *A* attempts to feint with a low round kick, he finds the Ving Tsun practitioner countering with a real attack.

C) Partner *A's* feinted high punch causes partner *B* to react defensively and suffer the subsequent sidekick to the ribs.

D) Partner *A* attempts the feinted punch and sidekick combo on the Ving Tsun practitioner. Unfortunately, this only provokes partner *B* into counterattacking aggressively.

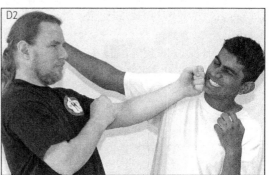

Ving Tsun: Combining Actual and Relative Speed

A system can be defined as "a regularly interacting or interdependent group of items forming a unified whole" (Merriam-Webster, 2011). By design, systems tend to exhibit qualities not possessed by the sum of their constituent parts, and in the case of military and security systems, they typically possess multiple levels of redundancy to ensure reliability.

As a system of martial arts, Ving Tsun gongfu meets all of these criteria. The relaxation and muscular conditioning taught in the Ving Tsun forms fuel the ability to move at high rates of actual speed. These two factors also engender the elastic, whiplash force used when striking and the proprioception employed when defending. This emphasis on elastic force also allows the practitioner to respond rapidly to tactile pressures as developed with *chisau* (sticking hands/arm clinging) training. In turn, chi sau training reinforces the importance of targeted muscle relaxation, which is critical for borrowing the opponent's force while preventing him from borrowing yours. Coming full circle, that same relaxation is what helped form the basis for actual speed in the first place. Taking these factors into account, consider that the physical techniques of Ving Tsun are typically applied at close range, contain no wasted motions, and comprise angles that are biomechanically strong. By incorporating superior timing and relative speed, Ving Tsun takes an art that is already extremely fast and makes it faster. In essence, not only does the Ving Tsun practitioner take a shortcut to the finish line, but he runs at full speed the entire way.

Conclusion

Considered separately, actual speed and relative speed are both important aspects of the martial arts. Yet when successfully combined, they give the practitioner a distinct advantage over his opponents. Physical limitations, genetics, muscular conditioning, and relaxation are the factors that affect one's potential for actual speed. Timing, structure, and position are the key factors affecting relative speed, and these can generally be learned by anyone regardless of physical potential. Ving Tsun gongfu is a system of martial arts that takes a very pragmatic view of fighting and self-defense. Of key concern is the need to end an altercation with absolute speed and efficiency. By offering a training method that combines high rates of actual speed with superior strategies for relative speed, Ving Tsun stands as a formidable system and fighting art.

Selected Ving Tsun Mottos Illustrated in this Article

Motto	Characters	Cantonese	Mandarin
1	連消帶打	*lin siu dai da*	*lian xiao dai da*
2	打手即消手	*da sau jik siu sau*	*da shou ji xiao shou*
3	後發先至	*hau fat sin ji*	*hou fa xian zhi*
4	一點攻擊	*yat dim kung kek*	*yi dian gong ji*
5	敵不動我不動	*dik but dung ngoh but dung*	*di bu dong wo bu dong*
	敵壹動我先動	*dik yat dung ngoh ji dung*	*di yi dong wo xian dong*

Other Mottos

	Characters	Cantonese	Mandarin
	打头無腳	*da tau mo gerk*	*da tou wu jiao*
	追形不手	*jiu ying but jiu sau*	*zhui xing bu shou*

Glossary

Characters	Cantonese	Mandarin	English Equivalent
膀手	*bongsau*	*bangshou*	wing hand/arm
黐手	*chisau*	*chishou*	sticky hands/ arm clinging
耕打	*gaun da*	*geng da*	ploughing hand + strike
耕手	*gaunsau*	*gengshou*	ploughing hand
剛	*gong*	*gang*	hard, rigid force
撳打	*gum da*	*qin da*	pinning hand + strike
撳手	*gumsau*	*qinshou*	pinning hand
拳訣	*kuen kuit*	*quan jue*	boxing mnemonic
拉手	*lapsau*	*lashou*	pulling hand
拍打	*pak da*	*pai da*	slapping hand + strike
拍手	*paksau*	*paishou*	slapping hand
劈打	*pat da*	*pi da*	hacking hand + strike
小念頭	*sil lim tao*	*xiao nian tou*	Little Idea
詠春拳	*ving tsun kuen*	*young chun quan*	ving tsun, wing chun, yong chun
柔	*yao*	*rou*	soft, flexible force

Acknowledgements

Special thanks to the following: Jason Miller for his photographic skills; Dr. Larry Brown and Harry Lundell for reviewing the final copy; Robert George, James Crull, Andrew Lucchesi, Jason Miller, and Gops Sethurathinam for assisting with the technique demonstrations.

Bibliography

Cheng, Man-ch'ing, and Smith, R. (1967). *T'ai-chi: The "supreme ultimate" exercise for health, sport, and self-defense.* (6th ed.). Rutland, VT: Charles E. Tuttle.

Hamilton, N. and Luttgens, K. (2002). *Kinesiology: Scientific basis of human motion.* New York: McGraw-Hill.

Kernspecht, K. (2004). *Der letze wird der erste sein: Das geheimnis effektiver selbstverteidigung.* [The last shall be first: The secret of effective self-defense]. Burg/Fehmarn: Wu Shu Verlag Kernspecht.

Kernspecht, K. (1987). *Vom zweikampf.* [On single combat]. (4th ed.). Burg/ Fehmarn: Wu Shu Verlag Kernspecht.

Kieser, W. (2003). *Ein starker körper kennt keinen schmerz.* [A strong body knows no pain]. (6th ed.). München: Wilhelm Heyne Verlag.

Nakayama, M. (1966). *Dynamic karate: Instruction by the master.* (19th ed.). New York: Kodansha International Ltd.

Speed. (2011). Merriam-Webster.com. Merriam-Webster Incorporated. Retrieved February 24, 2011, from http://www.merriam-webster.com/ dictionary/speed

System. (2011). Merriam-Webster.com. Merriam-Webster Incorporated. Retrieved February 24, 2011, from http://www.merriam-webster.com/ dictionary/system

Webb, J. (2007). Analysis of the wing tsun punching methods. *Journal of Asian Martial Arts, 16*(2), 62–81.

Webb, J. (2009). Tactile reflex development through wing tsun's "sticking hands" practice. *Journal of Asian Martial Arts, 18*(2), 44–59.

chapter 5

Tactile Reflex Development Through Wing Tsun's "Sticking Hands" Practice

by Jeff Webb

All photos courtesy of Jeff Webb.

Introduction

Two practitioners face each other, with both arms in contact with those of their partner. The two pairs of arms roll together in unison, rhythmically, and almost hypnotically, as each maintains precise positioning and spring-like pressure toward its counterpart. Sporadically, the practitioners will pause as one executes a simple attack with the palm or fist, probing for an opening or lack of attentiveness. The defender responds calmly to the attack by subtly deflecting it, after which, both practitioners return to their previous rolling-arms exercise. Sensing an opportunity, the other practitioner initiates a similarly simple, yet probing attack. As with his partner's attempt, this does not go unnoticed and the other quickly counters before both partners resume their rolling-arms exercise. The pace of this back-and-forth probing of each other's defenses

71

soon accelerates with one partner deciding to apply a more aggressive attack. While simultaneously controlling his partner's right arm with one hand, he attacks with the other, all in coordination with a very deep forward step. His partner, yielding passively to this attack, turns to the side to deflect it and then launches a counterattack. This attack is, in turn, countered and a response is issued, leading to a series of attacks, defenses, and counterattacks that culminate when one partner is unable to keep up the pace. Forced to acknowledge that blows are being landed to which he cannot adequately respond, he admits defeat. Ultimately, both practitioners will analyze where things broke down and will begin the process anew with the aim of correcting previous errors and extending the exchange of attacking and defending techniques.

A seasoned martial artist having witnessed this exchange might naturally question both the purpose and ultimate value of such an exercise. "Impressive, but that's not the way we spar," or "Great, but no one on the street will do that funny arm-rolling thing before a fight," or even, "Maybe you can do this with your own students, but how about practitioners of other styles?" All are valid questions. Primarily though, they stem from a lack of understanding as to the purpose of what they have just witnessed. It was not a sparring match nor was it a simulated street fight; rather it was a complex reflex training method. A method that is both counterintuitive and yet demonstrably effective.

Bruce Lee introduced wing tsun (wing chun, ving tsun, yong chun) gongfu's "sticking hands" (chisau)[1] exercise to the US during the 1964 Long Beach International Karate Championships. Forty-four years later, very few outside of the art truly understand chisau's purpose let alone how it develops tactile reflexes, that is, those reflexes based on pressure sensitivity and not what is seen. This article will describe both the fundamental and complex methods of chisau training in detail. It will also explain the rationale and theories behind the method as well as discuss a variety of factors that can either improve or retard the acquisition of tactile reflexes. For purposes of simplicity, we will use the term "tactile reflexes" to refer to those that are triggered by both pressure and touch.

Responses Arising from Visual & Tactile Stimuli

In the martial arts, there are two types of reflexes that can be differentiated by the type of stimuli that produces them. Visually cued reflexes are those whose origination begins with the eyes perceiving movement, followed by the transmission of visual data to the cerebral cortex for analysis, and culminating in one or more limbs being called upon to respond to the attack. In kinesiology, this type of reflex is called *exteroceptive* since the stimulus occurs externally of the human body. Another equally descriptive term for this would be *heteroceptive*, since the two components of the reflex arc,[2] the receptor (sensory) organ and the effector (motor response) organ, are distinct from one another.

On the other hand, tactilely cued reflexes are those initiated by physical contact with the body and yield an instantaneous and often subconscious physical response. Kinesiologists call these *proprioceptive reflexes* because the stimulus mechanisms that initiate them are internal of the human body. In this case, the receptor and effector organs are typically one and the same. Specifically, we are referring to four types of receptor organs or "proprioceptors" situated within the muscles and tendons: the Pacinian corpuscles, Ruffini endings, the muscle spindle, and the Golgi tendon organ.

These four proprioceptors function to constantly monitor both the position and movements of the human body. Being located within the muscles, tendons and joints gives them accurate real-time data on the intensity, direction, and duration of any pressure being applied against a martial artist when his limbs are in contact with those of his opponent.

Essentially, the key difference between visually and tactilely cued reflexes is the number of synapses[3] involved in the execution of a movement. In layman's terms, visually cued reflexes can be said to require three stations (the eyes, the higher brain, and the responding limb), while tactilely cued reflexes require only the limb itself (for both perception and response) and the nervous system (i.e. the spinal cord).[4]

Responses based on tactile cues are processed much faster since there are fewer organs and synaptic "stoplights" involved and because the task of responding is activated by the same sensory organ that processed the data in the first place. In a martial context, if one were able to make use of this sensory input and respond appropriately, the advantages would be numerous. The wing tsun chisau exercise offers a systematic training method for doing just that. By programming the limbs and body to respond in a certain fashion to certain pressures, chisau puts the body's tactile reflexes to work for the martial artist.

With wing tsun gongfu as with other martial arts, visually cued reflexes are utilized at a distance. Naturally, seeing a punch or kick coming at us is a necessary pre-requisite for making limb-to-limb contact in hopes of defending it. In this respect, wing tsun is no different than other approaches, yet wing tsun (WT) takes this a step further. A WT practitioner's goal is to first make limb-to-limb contact—often referred to as a "bridge"—and then to rely on the properly trained tactilely cued reflexes to respond appropriately to that contact. By using this tactile input and letting the limb both detect and redirect attacks, overall reaction time can be greatly reduced. Not only that, but the defensive movement's accuracy is enhanced when we allow our tactile reflexes to respond rather than by trying to make a conscious decision based on what we see. To put it another way, the limb that makes contact with an attack is in the best position to assess which defensive measure to apply; rather than choosing beforehand based only on visual observation. Visually, we cannot precisely know the angle, velocity, and power of an oncoming attack. Nor can we be 100% sure if it is real or feigned.

For this reason, wing tsun is based on four key fighting principles:

- When the way is free, **go forward**.
- If the way is obstructed, **stick to your opponent**.
- If you encounter greater force, **give way**.
- When the opponent withdraws or retreats, **follow through**.

Teaching the body to respond according to these principles is the goal of chisau training. While these four concepts are very simple, and wing tsun's approach to training them systematic, the underlying physiology that makes them work is still intriguing.

Kinesiology's Yin and Yang

The muscular control that enables us to stand, walk, manipulate objects, and maintain our balance is facilitated by a line of constant communication from the muscles and joints to the nervous system. This communication stems from two pairs of aforementioned proprioceptors: the muscle spindle and Golgi tendon organ, and the Pacinian corpuscles and Ruffini endings. Muscle spindles are located throughout the muscles and in greater concentrations at their core. They respond to changes in the length of a muscle as well as to how quickly or slowly these changes occur, giving rise to the stretch reflex. Imagine that a muscle is stretched while in the process of trying to contract. The spindles relay this data to the nervous system, which responds by causing the muscle to contract even more forcefully while simultaneously causing the opposing muscle group to relax. An example of this is when someone hands you a heavy box and, in anticipation, you reach forward with arms outstretched. Suddenly as the weight is transferred to your arms, you realize the box is much heavier than expected. At this point, your biceps start to extend and lengthen as you begin to lose your hold. When this happens, the stretch reflex takes over. Sensing the sudden lengthening of your biceps as they struggle to contract, the muscle spindles relay this to your nervous system. The result is a command from the nervous system that causes the biceps to contract more powerfully and the opposing triceps muscles to relax. Thus your body generates the extra strength needed to manage the heavy box and it does not get dropped. From this example, we can see that the stretch reflex gives us additional strength to perform a task.

On the other hand, the Golgi tendon organ causes exactly the opposite response. Situated at the insertion point of skeletal muscle fibers to the tendons, the Golgi tendon organ gives rise to the tendon reflex that can effectively override the stretch reflex if needed. When muscular contraction becomes too great and musculoskeletal damage is imminent, the tendon reflex causes the muscles to relax, thereby easing the pressure. In this fashion, the tendon reflex is a type of pressure safety valve that causes the muscles to give way before damage is done to muscles, tendons, and/or joints.

Next we come to the Pacinian corpuscles and Ruffini endings, which are found in abundance near the joint capsules. The Pacinian corpuscles monitor pressure applied to the joint capsule as well as any sudden changes in joint angle. However, they only monitor phasic changes in pressure. The Ruffini endings, which can also respond to abrupt changes in joint angle, serve to monitor continuous pressure on the joint. It is said that the Ruffini endings can detect even a 2% change in the angle of a joint.

Chisau training harnesses these four proprioceptive processes and marries them with martial techniques. The result enables a WT practitioner to respond quickly and accurately upon contact with their opponent's limbs.

Stretch Reflex Sequence

This sequence illustrates the stretch reflex. Partner *A* prepares to receive a heavy box from Partner *B*. As *B* hands him the box, *A* is unprepared. Surprised, *A* begins to lose hold of the box. At this moment, the stretch reflex activates. *A* regains his grip on the box and adjusts his posture.

Jeff Webb with double-knives.

Wing Tsun Chisau and Its Purpose

Although most often associated with double-arm (*sheung chisau*), chisau actually encompasses a wide variety of single- and double-arm exercises that focus on the development of acute tactile reflexes and sensitivity. While some feel that chisau training's goal is to teach hand trapping, this is a somewhat limited view. The ability to trap the opponent's hands is simply a by-product of chisau training and not the goal per se. The chisau training's actual goals are three-fold:

1) Provide a back-up system for failed attacks
2) Facilitate striking
3) Develop the ability to deflect and borrow the opponent's force

Consider the following example of a "bridge" made during a typical fight: Partner X launches a punch that Partner Y counters with a block. At this point, X's strike and Y's block are in contact and a bridge has been made. Following this, most martial arts generally teach the withdrawal of the attacking limb so that a subsequent move can be applied with the other. In wing tsun, however, the practitioner would "stick" when this bridge is made.

The benefits of this are two-fold: first, it allows the WT practitioner to keep one of the opponent's limbs in check. Essentially, the opponent couldn't even move that limb without the WT practitioner being aware of it, and take countermeasures. Second, keeping the opponent's limb(s) under control facilitates the WT practitioner's further attempts to strike.

Perhaps chisau training's most important function is the development of the ability to borrow the opponent's force and turn it against them. Strictly speaking, wing tsun doesn't teach blocks. Blocking implies that an attack is stopped, i.e., prevented from continuing its motion. On the contrary, wing tsun focuses on deflecting an opponent's attack by using a lesser force to off-load a greater force.

Underlying Concepts to Tactile Reflex Development

The proper training of tactile reflexes with chisau lies in understanding five key concepts: 1) active/passive roles, 2) proper structure, 3) forward pressure, 5) relaxation, and 5) sticking.

Understanding the concept of active and passive roles in tactile reflex training is perhaps the most important of the five and is the determining factor as to whether actual progress will be made. In a given training scenario, the active partner is the one who is attacking while the passive partner is the one who defends. During an actual fight, just as in chisau training, the two combatants would alternate between attacking and defending roles based on the actions of their opponent. If Partner A initiates an attack, then Partner B must defend and counter. Subsequently, Partner A must now defend before he can return fire.

However, as seen in fights between untrained combatants, each will swing wildly at the other in an attempt to maintain the active role throughout the fight. Unfortunately this comes at a heavy price. By attempting to attack without any type of defense, both combatants will end up bloodied and equally worse for the wear. Perhaps in the distant past, this realization dawned upon some primitive warrior and thus the concept of defense was born. However it began, acknowledgement of the passive role and, therefore, the need to defend became a key component in the martial arts.

Therefore, the passive role serves the purpose of allowing the martial artist to take the proverbial "one step backward" to take "two steps forward." In wing tsun, when we make a bridge with a much larger and stronger opponent, the necessity to give way is academic. Yet there are two paths we can choose. One is to give way involuntarily as we struggle to use our own brute strength, denying that we are out-matched until the very end. This typically results in getting struck and injured. The other is to give way voluntarily, which systematically allows us to borrow his strength and use it against him. Too often, beginners in chisau will attempt to rely on their own strength and brute force. Initially, this will serve them well against others of a similarly low level of skill. However, against a more skilled albeit weaker opponent, the person relying on power will generally find themselves clumsy, slower, and easily exploited. Brute strength works well unless you are up against someone who can, through skill, turn it against you. For this reason, each WT practitioner must learn to acknowledge the passive role to improve their own defensive skills, otherwise, they will remain at a rather mediocre skill level and never progress.

Proper Structure

Structure and positioning is paramount to the development of solid tactile reflexes. Just as proper structure is necessary to create bridges that can safely support the traffic that crosses them, it is equally important when we make the previously mentioned limb-to-limb bridge with our opponent. Correct angles and the positioning of both limbs and stance enable a WT practitioner to use minimal effort to achieve the maximum effect.

Maintaining Constant Forward Pressure

In chisau training, each partner will learn to give constant and flowing forward pressure toward their opponent. This forward pressure is applied by the arms and is generated primarily by the elbows, hence the term "elbow force." Additionally, it is supported by the stance and footwork when the body is put into motion. Upon making a bridge with the opponent's arms, forward pressure serves two distinct purposes: First, it allows one to maintain contact with the opponent's limbs and thereby detect any movement. Second, this pressure can be used to smother the enemy's power and keep them from gaining momentum as they attempt to move. A wing tsun practitioner will go forward, making a bridge (if the way is obstructed), and stick to the opponent's attacks, using forward pressure like a lead blanket to slightly muffle the opponent's speed and power.

Opinions vary from one instructor to the next on the amount of forward pressure needed. However, according to Kernspecht: "When a fighter's limbs establish contact with chisao ('clinging arms'), the question arises of how strong his own forward pressure should be. Owing to the sensory considerations, the answer to this question is to be found in the Steven's Power Function: the greater the pressure applied to the opponent's limb, the greater must be the difference between one's own pressure and the adversary's pressure before the latter's pressure can be sensed" (Kernspecht, 1987).

In other words, he advocates that your initial pressure should be quite light to enable quicker detection and interpretation of your opponent's movements. For real-world application this is absolutely true. When instructing an overly muscular or stiff beginner, however, the use of very heavy forward pressure is often necessary to get them to begin feeling pressure. By definition, muscle tone is residual muscular contraction, and an excess of this can impede the development of tactile reflexes. Therefore, in these instances, the instructor must often exert heavier pressure on the beginning student to illicit the proper yielding and responses. Over time, the diligent student will learn to relax their limbs and the basic motor reflexes will gradually take shape. The once inflexible student will then become more fluid, more relaxed, and quicker to respond to their partner's force. Generally though, this excessive pressure is only for the purpose of helping the stiffer student achieve flexibility and is not how one would attempt to perform chisau with a training partner. Quite the contrary, whether during chisau practice or actual combat, one should closely follow Mr. Kernspecht's advice and maintain a very light touch upon initial contact. By sticking with light pressure, we maximize our ability to perceive and respond as quickly as possible. In actual application, anything in excess of this not only impedes one's tactile sensitivity, but gives a skillful opponent enough force to use against you.

Relaxation

Relaxation is the key to wing tsun's third principle of giving way. In chisau, the arms are kept loose and relaxed with only the needed muscles being contracted, and then only when necessary. For example, while practicing the rolling-arms exercise, only the muscles needed to hold position and generate light forward pressure are used. The others remain relaxed yet ready to be used at any time. Relaxation is an important compliment to forward pressure in that it acts as a kind of relief valve. This allows one to give way or off-load the force of the opponent when it becomes too great. Additionally, a certain degree of relaxation is necessary, per Steven's Power Function, for quickly detecting pressure and direction changes.

Sticking

What we term as sticking in wing tsun is a function of the two previous concepts working together. If the opponent suddenly withdrew their arm, forward pressure would allow us to stick and follow. Yet if they abruptly pushed forward against us, it is relaxation that would allow us to give way and maintain both contact and control of their limb. In combination, the forward pressure and relaxation give one's arms the properties of a spring. The spring will contract when compressed and extend when released. Its pressure from our arms is constant, yet its intensity fluctuates in direct response to the amount of pressure exerted against us.

Cross-Arm Single Sticking Hand

The most basic of the single-arm chisau exercises is the cross-arm chisau. *A* (left) puts his right arm in a low wing arm position, while *B* grabs his wrist. *A* changes his wing arm to a sinking hand. With *B*'s arm turned, *A* changes his hand into a shocking hand to fully break his grip. Now *A* attacks with a finger thrust toward *B*'s face. *B* maintains forward pressure and sticks to *A*'s arm with his own finger thrust. At this point, *A* will grasp *B*'s wrist and pull it downward, which causes them to reverse roles as they repeat the sequence.

Overhead view: 1

1

2

2

3

3

4

4

Fundamental Reflex Training

The basic chisau reflex training begins with single-arm exercises and later progresses to more complex double-arm exercises. Our development as human beings requires that we must learn to stand before learning to walk, and that we must be able to walk before learning to run. In a similar way, single-arm exercises are a necessary prerequisite to learning the double-arm exercises. Although the single-arm exercises lack the excitement of the more advanced double-arm drills, they nonetheless build the foundational responses that make the double-arm maneuvers possible. Bruce Lee reportedly asked "how long must I practice this [expletive] until I learn how to fight?" Whether or not this is true, the handful of videos showing Lee's liquidity and speed while performing chisau are a testament to the results. Experience has shown that students who diligently practice single-arm chisau tend to progress much quicker in the double-arm exercises than those who neglect these foundational skills.

The first of the single-arm exercises, the crossed single-arm chisau, initiates the student to the concepts of active and passive roles, forward pressure, and sticking to their partner's arm. The techniques used in the basic cycle of movements are sinking hand (*jamsau*), jerking hand (*jutsau*), finger-thrusting hand (*biujisau*), and wing arm (*bongsau*). Both partners will maintain limb-to-limb contact as they cycle through the movements in rote fashion. Emphasis is placed on keeping the arms relaxed and exerting slight forward pressure during the repetitions.

After sufficient progress is made with the crossed single-arm chisau, the student will begin learning the parallel single-arm chisau exercise. The movements used in this exercise are controlling arm (*fooksau*), sinking arm, the straight-line punch, spreading hand (*tansau*), erect palm strike, and wing arm. As with the crossed single-arm exercise, the two partners will work on maintaining pressure toward each other's center while keeping the arms as relaxed as possible.

Once the student can perform the basic cycle fluidly, additional dimensions are added to the parallel single-arm chisau exercise, including responses to attacks coming from three different levels and those that integrate footwork. In the three-level variation, the partner performing the straight-line punch can vary between low, middle, and high targets. The partner will respond accordingly with low wing arm, middle (or standard) wing arm, or high punch according to circumstances. At this point, the standard rote responses can be randomized based on the partner's attack. In order to get the most out of this exercise, it is essential that the instructor (or training partner) avoid being predictable when applying the low, middle, or high level attacks. If the attacks come in a predictable sequence the student may respond accordingly, but are reacting to a pattern and not to spontaneous attacks. This is contrary to the true purpose of chisau training, which is to respond accurately to the unpredictability of an opponent.

Following the three-level exercise, students will learn to integrate their hand skills with footwork. The sequences involving the punch and the erect palm are then applied in conjunction with the advancing step (*chin bo*). In response to the advancing punch, the partner will apply a stance turn and wing arm; whereas in response to the palming attack, they will learn to use the sinking arm technique in coordination with the stance turn.

When all of the single-arm chisau drills have been mastered, the student's basic reflexes will be smooth and accurate. They will have competence in the use of the single arm to defend high or low attacks or mid-level attacks coming in any combinations. Further, they will have learned to deflect an opponent's advancing attack by using the stance turn as a pressure relief valve. Now the student is ready to move onto the double-arm chisau exercises, which will become a staple of their training regimen for the rest of their career as a wing tsun practitioner.

詠春拳

Wing Tsun Kuen (Cantonese)
Yong Chun Quan (Mandarin)

Parallel-Arm Single Sticking Hand
This exercise is somewhat more difficult than the cross-arm version.

A (left) uses the spreading hand and *B* uses the controlling arm. *A* initiates an attack with the palm. *A* defends passively with a sinking arm. *B* now takes the active role and attacks with a punch, while *A* defends passively with wing arm. Both partners resume their original positions and then repeatedly cycle through the exercise. *B* could also have attacked with a high punch, which *A* would defend with a punch of his own. *B* could also have attacked with a lower punch, which *A* would defend with a low wing arm.

Overhead view.

Complex Reflex Training Using Both Arms

As a whole, the chisau exercises are perhaps one of the most ingenious training methods known. Although numerous refinements and improvements have been made by different instructors over the centuries, wing tsun gongfu founders (purportedly 250-300 years ago) were among the most intelligent scholar-warriors of their time. The founders of this training method seem to have had an advanced understanding of neurophysiology, psychology, kinesiology, physics, and geometry. Nowhere else is this more obvious than with double-arm chisau training.

In double-arm chisau, the practitioner will learn to use both arms to simultaneously perform coordinated tasks in response to tactile stimuli. Typically, while one arm is defending, the other is counterattacking. But quite often, both arms will process and react to tactile stimuli independently of one another. To fully understand the level of reflex and skill required to do this, consider the classic "pat your head and rub your stomach" test. For some, this reflex game is difficult enough and yet the movements involved are pre-planned. Now imagine moving the limbs as tactile-reflex responses to separate, random pressures applied against both arms at the same time.

One of the challenges that chisau training overcomes is the inherent hemispheric dominance of the brain, a factor that also determines a person's left-handedness or right-handedness. In chisau, the student is trained not only to be ambidextrous but to coordinate both arms in the performance of different tasks at the same time. For this reason, we refer to the double-arm chisau as complex training of the reflexes. It is important to clarify that wing tsun gongfu relies on simple and biomechanically sound body movements. So by complex we are speaking to the relative difficulty of coordinating the two arms and not the techniques themselves.

The first exercise of the double-arm chisau training is called rolling arms (*poonsau*). It begins with the arms of two training partners in contact. Both partners will position their left arms in the controlling arm (*fooksau*) position, while their right arms will alternate between the spreading hand (*tansau*) and wing arm (*bongsau*) positions throughout the exercise. In rolling arms, it is important that the "controlling arm" function as the impulse that essentially drives the exercise. As partner **A** pushes with his controlling arm against partner **B**'s spreading hand, the spreading hand will roll into a wing arm position. At the same time, partner **B**'s controlling arm will press against **A**'s wing arm causing it to shift into the spreading hand position. Having completed half a cycle, the partners will use their controlling arm to press in the opposite manner, thereby resuming their original positions.

By training in this manner, the controlling arm is the active limb while the spreading hand/wing arm is the passive limb. As in the single arm chisau exercises, acknowledging when to be active and when to be passive is essential to training the limbs to respond correctly. It is a mistake for either partner to apply the wing arm or spreading hand actively as these are meant to be passive reactions in both actual fighting and in chisau training. The more consistently a practitioner relies on their partner's force to cause their defense, the quicker and more reliably the reflexes will be programmed.

Rolling Arms

This exercise forms the platform from which all of the advanced chisau attacks and defenses are applied. *A* (left) puts his left hand in controlling arm position and his right in spreading arm position. *B* (right) puts his left hand in controlling arm and his right in wing arm. Both partners cycle and change arm positions in response to the pressure from the controlling arm. Now *A*'s right hand is in wing arm and *B*'s right hand is in spreading arm. The two partners will repeatedly "roll their arms," which gives the exercise its name.

Overhead view: I

I

Overhead view: 2

2

Yielding with Spreading Arm (Tan Sau)

By learning to yield to an opponent's force, a WT practitioner can effectively borrow the attacker's on-coming force to power his own counterattack.

LEFT: Spring Example #1: From chisau training, the practitioner's arms take on a spring-like reaction to pressure. *A* (left) presses *B*'s arm downward, it bends like a thin piece of rattan. Upon making contact with *A*'s hand, *B*'s arm will instantly begin giving counterpressure. When *A* quickly draws his hand back, *B*'s arm will spring upward.

RIGHT: Spring Example #2: As *B*'s arm is compressed, it will bend into a spreading arm position and upon further pressure his stance will also turn. However, when released, his arm will thrust forward and change into a punch.

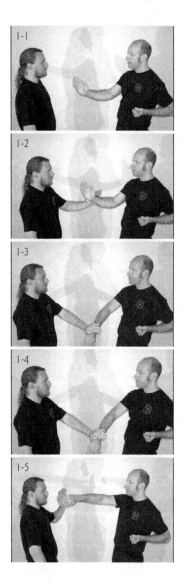 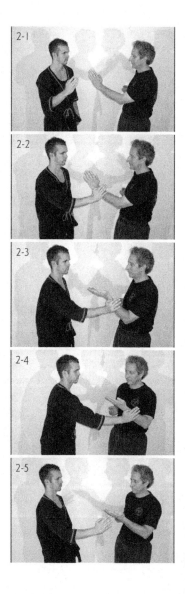

BELOW: Two partners square off. *B* steps forward and attacks with a straight-line punch. *A* counterattacks with a punch, which clashes against *B*'s punch. *B* yields to the on-coming force and changes his punch into a *tansau* while simultaneously launching a punch from the other hand.

Yielding with Wing Arm

Deflecting the opponent's force can leave them off balance and allows the wing tsun practitioner to flow quickly into the next movement. *A* (left) and *B* (right) face off. *B* advances with a straight-line punch, which *A* attempts to block. As *A*'s block presses down, *B*'s attacking arm yields to the pressure, changing to wing arm while the rear hand initiates a punch.

Defensive Responses

Left: Defensive response requiring one arm. Here the partner on the right is defending the punch with slapping hand (*paksau*).

Center: Defensive response requiring coordinated actions by two arms. In this situation, the partner on the right is defending with crossed rotating arms (*kwunsau*).

Right: Defensive response requiring independent actions by two arms. *A* defends a simultaneous two-pronged attack with a detaining hand (*kausau*) and low wing arm.

Rolling Arm Positions (Frontal View)

In the standard rolling arm exercise, both partners will alternate between controlling/spreading arm and spreading/wing arm. This pattern is referred to as Yin-Yang Hand, since each partner will have one hand at the inside position and one at the outside. In the double-hand rolling arm exercise, one partner will put both hands in controlling arm at the outside position while the other will use spreading/wing arm at the inside position.

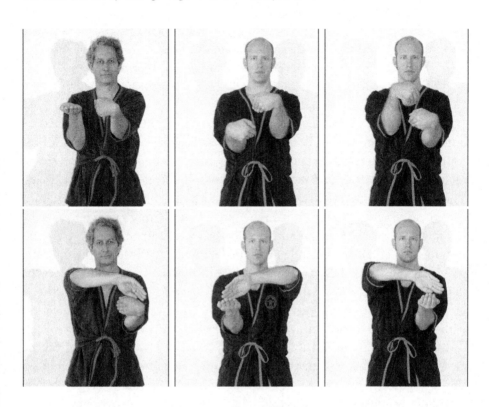

Following competence in performing rolling arms (*poonsau*), attacking techniques will be introduced into the training. This fighting practice in chisau is termed *kuosau*. It begins with the basic attacks from the single-arm chisau. As the two partners perform "rolling arms," one will initiate either a single-palm strike or punch. When this occurs, both partners will pause from rolling while the attack is defended, they will then resume the rolling-arms exercise. Later, the basic attacks will be applied with increasing frequency and intensity. In addition to this, the partners can alternate their hand positions between one hand inside and one hand outside, to one partner having both hands inside and the other with both hands outside. Hand changes from outside to inside and vice-versa are called *woon sau*. *Woon sau* trains the practitioner to readjust their position whenever their opponent makes a change as well as adding to the fluidity of the rolling-arms exercise.

At this stage, compound detaining hand (*kuo sau*) attacks are taught. These are attacks that involve using one arm to perform a controlling move while attacking with the other arm and executing an advancing step at the same time. In response to this type of attack, the defender must apply both hand techniques and footwork simultaneously. After the initial attack and defense, there will be numerous counterattacks and defenses that teach the practitioner three different types of responses:

1) Defensive responses requiring one arm
2) Defensive responses requiring coordinated actions by two arms, and
3) Defensive responses requiring independent actions by two arms

The process of teaching these compound attacks and advanced reflexes is broken down into sections. Each section generally consists of a basic attack from rolling arms, a defense to that attack, a counterattack, one or more cycles of repeating movements, and techniques to enter and exit the repeating cycles. The sections are basically two-man forms, although the sequences contained within each section can be varied providing an element of randomness to the training. Once each chisau training section has been learned, the movements it contains can be integrated and randomized with previously learned sections to provide an almost endless variety of exchanges between two practitioners. The first seven sections deal with the technical knowledge contained in the *sil lim tao* (*siu lim tau*, little idea) and *chum kiu* (seeking the bridge) forms of wing tsun. Later sections deal with techniques contained in the *biutze* (*biujee*, thrusting fingers) form, and ultimately the *muk yan jong* (wooden dummy) form.

The basic chisau sections teach structure, proper technique, and foundational responses. As a practitioner advances in skill, he will be taught slightly different versions or variations of the basic sections. These permutations are essentially variations on a theme. In other words, they teach the student to deal with attacks that might appear different, yet come at them from angles or positions similar to those they have already learned to defend against. One example that can help clarify this thought is to consider basic stick strikes used in the Philippine art of escrima. In the escrima style that the author studied, there are 4 basic forehand or backhand strikes that come in at different angles (not including any stabbing or thrusting strikes, which comprise the fifth angle). The angles of these four strikes are roughly approximate to 2, 4, 8, and 10 o'clock. During a real fight, however, an attacker's strike will not always conform to these fixed angles. However, the attack will more closely approximate one angle or another. So in defending, the practitioner will adapt their own defense slightly to accommodate the variance. Therefore, it is learning to adapt to these gray areas that is the goal of the training. With time, experience, and ample practice, the student of chisau will become accustomed to dealing with attacks from any angle.

The variations on the basic chisau sections provide a systematic way to further train this adaptability. Typically, different instructors will have a preference for teaching one version or another as their basic (or standard) method. This is often confusing for the less experienced practitioner who may have learned it one way, only to meet another instructor whose preference is to do it differently. As advanced practitioners well know, personal preferences from one instructor or the next are minor issues. The goal of developing tactile reflexes that allow one to accurately respond and adapt to the movements of the opponent is the more important point.

Jeff Webb with double-knives.

Ante Perception vs. Tactile Sensitivity

The expert martial artist with many years of sparring experience often utilizes a skill of which they are not consciously aware: ante perception. In the context of martial arts, ante perception can be defined as alertness to subtleties in the positions or movements of an opponent that allow the experienced fighter to essentially predict and respond in advance of their opponent's attack. Typically, slight movements of the eyes, nose, head, hips, and shoulders as well as weight shifts from one leg to other, are visual cues veteran fighters learn to pick up on. Wing tsun's founders also recognized this phenomenon. An ancient wing tsun axiom states: "fight nose to nose, not nose to fist," and is applied to dealing with attacks such as roundhouse punches and turning kicks. Truly, ante perception can give the experienced fighter distinct advantages over novices, especially in martial arts that rely exclusively on visual cues.

However, as useful as this skill may be, there are some potential downsides. For one thing, the fighter who relies predominantly on ante perception is still subject to feints and sucker punches. In competition, seasoned tournament fighters will often study how their opponents react to certain movements or attacks and use this to their advantage. Likewise, the street thug who arguably has more real-world fighting experience than the average martial artist, would similarly be experienced in the pros and cons of ante perception, even if only at a subconscious level. Finally, ante perception is still based solely on visual information, which may function adequately at longer ranges, but is at a severe handicap at in-fighting range.

In contrast to ante perception, tactile sensitivity does not make predictions. Mechanical input, rather than visual, provides the basis for response. At very close range where attacks come quickly leaving little time for conscious decision-making during the fight, tactile sensitivity is far superior. Punches, elbow strikes, and knee strikes can be among the most damaging of close-range tactics. It is tactile sensitivity that offers a logical and systematic defense against them.

Conclusion

Chisau is a very comprehensive and systematic method of training tactile reflexes. Despite often being portrayed as mystical or even mythical, it is a method backed by solid science with concepts stemming from neurophysiology, psychology, kinesiology, physics, and geometry. The chisau training method is key to teaching wing tsun's main fighting principles by programming the limbs to go forward when the way is free, to stick and maintain contact if obstructed, to yield or give way when necessary, and ultimately to pursue the opponent relentlessly if they withdraw or retreat at all. The programming of tactile reflexes is accomplished through a series of single and double-arm exercises that increase in difficulty and specificity over time. By leveraging the use of various pre-wired physiological functions, chisau is far more than a rote drill or exercise. Finally, proper understanding of the concepts will enable both instructor and student to make quicker progress in a shorter period of time.

Notes

[1] The character for *sau* usually translates as "hand", but in wing tsun, it often makes more sense to translate as "arm" in English.

[2] The reflex arc is the physiological pathway of a reflex action. It is composed of at least two neurons with one being the afferent (sensory) neuron and the other the efferent (motor) neuron. The simplest and quickest reflex arcs are said to be monosynaptic, containing only one afferent neuron and one efferent neuron. Reflex arcs based on visual sensory data are always polysynaptic and may require many synapses.

[3] Synapses are essentially junctions where nerve impulses pass from one neuron to the next. Obviously the fewer synapses or "synaptic stoplights" involved, the quicker the reflex action.

[4] Most sensory neurons synapse in the spinal cord and are therefore processed very quickly (e.g. patellar reflex, flexor reflex, etc.). Visual sensory data passes from the eyes through the brain. Not only is this a polysynaptic process, but a conscious decision-making process occurs before a reflex action is initiated.

Character	Cantonese	Mandarin	English Equivalent
標指	biutze	biaozhi	thrusting fingers
標指手	biutzesau	biaozhishou	thrusting fingers/hands
膀手	bongsau	bangshou	wing hand/arm
黐手	chisau	chishou	sticking hand
尋橋	chum kiu	xun qiao	bridge seeking
單黐手	dan chisau	dan chishou	single sticking hand
伏手	fook sau	fu shou	controlling hand
箭步	chin bo	jian bu	arrow (advancing) step
沈手	jumsau	chenshou	sinking hand/arm
窒手	jutsau	zhishou	jerking hand
過手	kausau	guoshou	fighting hand
盤手	poonsau	panshou	rolling hand
雙黐手	sheung chisau	shuang chishao	double sticking hands
小念頭	sil lim tao	xiao nian tou	little idea form
攤手	tansau	tanshou	spreading palm hand/arm
換手	woonsau	huanshou	changing hand

Bibliography

Derse, E. (1993). *Explosive power: Plyometrics for bodybuilders, martial artists and other athletes*. Los Angeles: Health For Life.

Hamilton, N. and Luttgens, K. (2002). *Kinesiology: Scientific basis of human motion*. New York: McGraw-Hill.

Kernspecht, K. (2004). *Der letze wird der erste sein: das geheimnis effektiver selbstverteidigung*. [The last shall be first: The secret of effective self-defense]. Burg/Fehmarn: Wu Shu Verlag Kernspecht.

Kernspecht, K. (1987). *Vom zweikampf* [On single combat]. Burg/Fehmarn: Wu Shu Verlag Kernspecht.

Kurz, T. (1987). *Stretching scientifically: A guide to flexibility training*. Cypress: Stadion Publishing Co.

Acknowledgments

The author would like to thank several of his students for their assistance: Dr. Larry Brown and Harry Lundell, who proofread this article; and Alex McCarrier, Robert George, Michael Yarbrough, and Matt Mauldon for appearing with Dr. Brown in the photographs.

chapter 6

Slap-Spread, Pull-Hit:
Favorite Wing Chun Applications

by Joyotpaul Chaudhuri, Ph.D.

Where I Learned These Techniques

Augustine Fong was a top student of Ho Kamming of Macao, who studied for many years with Ip Man (1893-1972), the central figure in the spreading of Wing Chun (*Yong Chun*). I began studying at Fong's Wing Chun Academy in Tucson in 1976. To serious students, Fong teaches the complete art: its principles, concepts, forms, wooden dummy, weapons, hands-on practice, foundation-based techniques, and interactive application and adjustment to varying situations. Stability, mobility, sharp timing, spontaneous and reflexive action, relatively squared body, double handedness, understanding lines and angles, and coordinated usage of the entire body rather than excessive muscle tension are all features of good teaching and learning of the style.

Wing Chun has many techniques, but actual situations and opponents can vary so much that Wing Chun does not depend on fixed answers to fixed attacks. A situation can be handled in a variety of ways. Doing lots of Wing Chun tends to develop natural and spontaneous responses. But all techniques emerge from three fundamental arm positions: wing (*bong*), control (*fook*), and spreading (*tan*). These positionings allow one to protect the center line emerging from one's own body, particularly the central axis, from different directions and planes. Ideally, the positions also allow power to be directed to the other person's axis.

The two techniques or motions chosen for this article are the slapping-spreading combination (*pak-tan*), and the pulling-hitting combination (*lop-da*). To be successful with both—in addition to the timing practice of various kinds of sticky hands—it's important to master the stability of the Wing Chun stance and learning how to turn and step. The hand structures have to be integrated with the structures of the upper and lower body, connected by controlling the center point complex of the body (*dantian*). In Wing Chun structures, geometry plays a role. Triangles and their adjustment to circles are important.

Memorable Incidences

Years ago I used the slapping-spreading combination in controlling a powerful punch thrown by a burly attacker in a bus station. And I used it in moving in on a skilled kenpo person kicking at my head. With footwork I used the pulling-hitting combination in neutralizing a visiting grappler's attempt to take me down. These and other empirical experiences helped me to understand the effectiveness of learning good Wing Chun.

Tips on Practice

The development of the slapping-spreading combination requires the index fingers of the slapping and spreading hands to meet at the apex of a triangle, with both elbows forming the other two points. The elbows are sunk, but springy and strong. Upon or near contact, the slapping and spreading hands can spread to adjust to the incoming force while still using an adapted triangular formation. Understanding the range of the work and limits of the springing and appropriate circling qualities of all the joints (particularly the elbows, wrists, and knees) is important. My partner, Joshua Santobianco, is a powerful striker and a well-trained grappler who is well versed in Wing Chun. In the photographs taken by Dana Albert, I am shown adjusting the slapping-spreading combination to control the force of Joshua's strike.

The development of the pulling-hitting combination also involves the coordination of the *lop* (a grabbing motion) with the protective hand (*wu sao*). Again, the elbows help create a triangular formation of the forearms and hands. The grabbing motion can be used effectively in close-quarter control of the opponent at the point of contact: forearm, shoulder, and head are examples. In the photo (2b), I am shown controlling Josh's left-hand strike with a wing hand (*bong*) and a protective hand. The protective hand quickly turns into a grab (2c) by sinking the elbow, and the wing arm turns into a strike by swiveling the elbow. The two hands need to work together.

In using these two techniques, basic Wing Chun principles apply. Maintain your own structural balance, disturb the other person's, and control the center line connecting the axis of your structure with that of your opponent.

In good Wing Chun, if you can control your own balance—and your opponent's—you can do whatever you intend, including stopping an attack, striking, kicking, breaking, or throwing. With good practice, the two techniques discussed can perform all these functions. The final moves of each sequence (1e and 2e) illustrate the possibilities in controlling and breaking structures through the use of Wing Chun.

Following pages:
Chaudhuri's partner in action shots
is Joshua Santobianco.

Photography by Dana Albert.

TECHNIQUE 1: Pak-tan Combination

1a) Josh strikes; Joy readies to block with a left slapping hand and right spreading hand combination. 1b) Stepping in, Joy uses a left slapping with a right palm-up protective motion. 1c) The slapping palm controls Josh's structure via his elbow, and Joy's right executes a palm-up neck strike. 1d) Joy's right hand controls Josh while he strikes with his left palm down. 1e) Joy's left leg moves in to control Josh's knee, getting ready for a fast torquing and throwing Josh down to the ground.

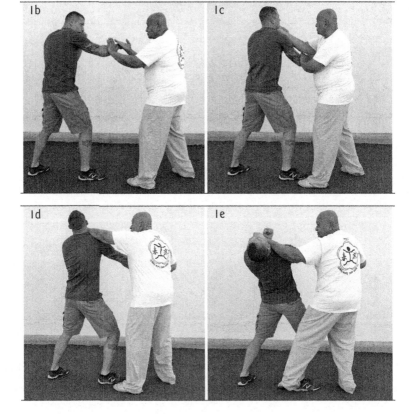

TECHNIQUE 2: Lop-da Combination

2a) Josh begins to strike. Joy prepares to make contact with his right wing forearm and positions a protective left hand. **2b)** Joy deflects and controls with the wing arm's contact point. **2c)** Shifting, Joy's protective hand grabs the wrist to control Josh and simultaneously chops Josh's neck with the right hand. **2d)** Joy folds Josh's left arm, trapping both hands while pulling his head down, breaking his structure and balance. **2e)** Joy continues to torque and knees Josh.

chapter 7

A Life-long Lesson in Ving Tsun Double-Knives

by Jeff Webb

Two weapon sets taught in Ving Tsun gongfu are the long-staff set known in Cantonese as *luk-dim-boon-gwun* (Mandarin *liudian ban gun fa*, 六點半棍法, meaning six-and-a-half-point pole) and the double-knives set called *bart-cham-do* in Cantonese (Mandarin: *ba zhan dao*, 八斬刀, meaning eight cutting blades). Considered advanced instruction, these are taught only to practitioners who have already mastered the empty-hand aspects of the system.

As a former student of Grandmaster Leung Ting, the closed-door disciple of the late Grandmaster Yip Man, I consider myself fortunate to have studied the weapons under his instruction and additionally with some of my gongfu brothers. It is well known that Yip Man highly regarded the double-knives techniques and taught the whole form to not more than four people in his lifetime. Among these, Leung is widely regarded as his most accomplished student in this area.

Owing to the somewhat exclusive nature of Ving Tsun weapons training and to the itinerant lifestyle of my former teacher, each lesson on the weapons was a memorable one. As a general rule, lessons on the weapons were always private or at least semiprivate in nature. Over the years, my weapons instruction took place in no less than six different cities and at venues ranging from martial arts schools to hotel rooms and balconies.

Yet my fondest memories are of my very first weapons lesson, which took place in San Antonio, Texas, back in 1988. At that time, my gongfu brother Gilbert Leal was hosting a general seminar by our teacher and had invited a select few to attend an additional session that was held afterward. The topic was the double-knives routine.

Though we were only taught one practice sequence that day (shown in photos 1a–5a), it was a rare opportunity and therefore the most meaningful for a young student. Only years later, when I formally learned the weapons, would I realize these movements were derived from the first two sections of the double-knives form. The sequence shown in photos 1b–5b is an application of movements from the fifth section of the form.

In the double-knives set, as in empty-hand Ving Tsun, good footwork is essential. Beyond being merely a delivery system for our techniques, Ving Tsun footwork is a method of moving the body as a unit to augment the execution of those techniques. Therefore, the double-knives set places great emphasis on coordinating the knife movements with body shifting and momentum for both offensive and defensive gain.

A practical example of this is the knife technique used to deal with long weapons. When facing an opponent armed with a long pole or a spear, the knife practitioner will employ advanced footwork to quickly bridge the gap and get in close. At this short range, the enemy's longer weapon is rendered unwieldy and thus is a disadvantage. For this reason, footwork practice is at the top of the list when it comes to improving your proficiency with the double-knives set. In addition, the following three areas are important:

▶ **Correct Mindset:** Weapons training must be approached with the proper mindset. The weapons techniques were developed during a historical period when real combat skills meant the difference between life and death. In Ving Tsun there is a saying: "Fear the younger opponent in fist fighting; fear the older [more experienced] opponent in weapons fighting." Being struck during an empty-hand fight is not necessarily fatal, but in weapons fighting, every blow landed is potentially crippling, if not lethal. Therefore, weapons practice should always be performed with a serious attitude.

▶ **Realistic Practice:** Once the movements can be performed at normal speed, one should begin practicing them with increasing speed and power. This extends to both the forms training and the practical applications against an opponent. Defending against weapons at walk-through pace is not enough; training at functional speed is essential to developing functional skills.

▶ **Repetition, Repetition, Repetition:** Upon beginning my formal weapons training in early 2002, my teacher said something that has stuck with me ever since. He said that all too often, after a student has learned the weapons, that student spends little actual time practicing them. For many, the prestige of acquiring the weapons knowledge is more important than practicing and getting good at them. The one notable exception was his senior European student, Keith R. Kernspecht, whom he candidly stated was his best student of the weapons, owing to Kernspecht's long-term, continual practice. It should be obvious that facility and expertise come not from just a few hundred repetitions, but from thousands.

Improving one's skills at anything in life can be done by applying these same principles. Approach things with a correct mindset, practice in a realistic fashion, and above all remember that it takes repetition to make the master.

Technique I

la) Jeff Webb faces an opponent armed with a wooden bat. **lb)** As the opponent steps in and swings, Webb steps forward at an angle, simultaneously contacting the attacker's hand and throat with the "dragging knives" (*tal-do*) technique. **lc–e)** Webb quickly follows up with the chain stabbing technique to the torso.

Technique 2

2a) Webb faces an opponent wielding a heavy machete. **2b)** As the attacker swings downward, Webb makes contact with the "asking knife" (*man-do*) technique. **2c)** Guiding the machete past him as he advances, Webb counters with a "throat-cutting knife" (*shat-geng-do*) technique. **2d)** The attacker drops his weapons and collapses, but not before receiving additional stabbing attacks to the torso.

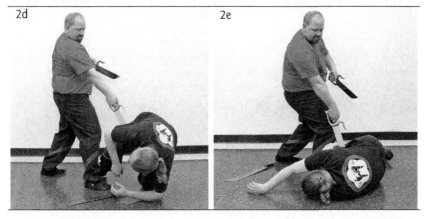

index

Printed in Great Britain
by Amazon

46087233R00059